The Way Forward

D

The Way Forward

Dr Mahathir bin Mohamad

Weidenfeld & Nicolson
LONDON

First published in Great Britain in 1998
by Weidenfeld & Nicolson
The Orion Publishing Group Ltd
Orion House
5 Upper Saint Martin's Lane
London WC2H 9EA

© 1998 Dr Mahathir Mohamad

A CIP catalogue record for this book is available
from the British Library.

ISBN 0 297 84229 3

Typeset by Selwood Systems, Midsomer Norton
Printed by Butler & Tanner Ltd
Frome and London

CONTENTS

The Way Forward

I

The New Economic Policy

Where some people are very wealthy and others have nothing, the result will be either extreme democracy or absolute oligarchy, or despotism will come from either of those excesses.

Aristotle (384–322 BC)

The Historical Background

On 13 May 1969 racial riots broke out in the Malaysian capital of Kuala Lumpur. Trouble was not entirely unexpected. There had always been bad blood between the Malays and Chinese, in part due to them not knowing each other, the two races having been kept apart by the 'divide and rule' policy of the British colonial government. The Malays and Chinese were also completely different, with their own distinct ethnic, language, cultural and religious affiliations. In the days following the end of the Second World War, Chinese communist guerrillas, bitterly anti-Japanese and seeing in the Japanese surrender an opportunity to seize political power in the Malay Peninsula, attacked Malay villagers in several parts of the countryside and seized a number of police stations. The Malays retaliated in kind and became even more anti-Chinese in the immediate years that followed.

The British proposal, announced two months after the end of the war, to confer citizenship on all the people resident in the Malay states and the Straits Settlements,[1] as part of a newly formed Malayan Union, a plan hatched in Whitehall during the Japanese Occupation of what was then Malaya, did nothing to improve relations between the two communities. The Malays felt that the British were being generous to the Chinese at their expense. They doubted the loyalty of the Chinese to the Malay states, and consequently to the proposed Malayan Union, especially when the British raised no objections to them holding dual citizenship of China and Malaya.

[1] During the years of British colonial rule the three settlements of Penang, Melaka and Singapore were known as the Straits Settlements.

Nevertheless, relations between the Chinese and Malays appeared to have improved when, in 1955, the pre-independence federal elections in Malaya were won by the Alliance of the United Malays National Organisation (UMNO), the Malayan Chinese Association (MCA) and the Malayan Indian Congress (MIC), the three political parties representing the Malays, the Chinese and the Indians respectively.[2] This unique coalition of the principal ethnic groups in Malaysia was so successful that of the 52 seats contested, only a single seat went to one of the opposition parties, the Pan Malayan Islamic Party (PMIP), which was exclusively Malay. The Alliance candidates won because they could count on the support of all races, whereas the other parties contesting the elections drew their support from only one ethnic group.

Following their victory, the Alliance sent a multiracial delegation to London, led by UMNO President and Alliance leader, Tunku Abdul Rahman, to demand independence. The British Government, which had previously used the excuse that the Malays would not get along with the other races in order to delay independence, was no longer in a position to reject the demand. So independence was granted in 1957, two years earlier than the date originally insisted on by the British.

It seemed that political cooperation between the Malays and the Chinese was possible and viable. But in the early years of independence the Malays began to resent the continued Chinese domination of the economy. No studies were made at that time, but even a casual observer could not help noticing that the Malays had very little of the nation's wealth. They continued to be mostly peasant farmers and rubber smallholders, living from hand to mouth, with no role in the commercial activities of the country.

In fact, the biggest share of the nation's wealth was still in the

[2] The Malayan Chinese Association and the Malayan Indian Congress changed their names to the Malaysian Chinese Association (MCA) and the Malaysian Indian Congress (MIC) respectively following the creation of Malaysia in September 1963.

hands of foreigners, principally the former colonial power, the British. But Chinese business domination was more visible. They owned all the retail outlets, transport companies and distribution businesses. Their enterprises were family owned and employed almost exclusively Chinese staff. The towns were overwhelmingly Chinese, with all the business signboards written in big Chinese characters.

The Malays began to demand a share of the nation's wealth through participation in business and industry. They were dissatisfied with the rural development drive, initiated by the Alliance Government in an attempt to alleviate poverty in the outlying areas, where most Malays lived. They felt that they were being kept away from the real sources of wealth in their own country.

As the Malays formed the backbone of support for the Alliance Government, they expected the Government to correct the imbalances in the economic field, which had originated and been allowed to fester during the colonial period. Not seeing any improvement, a narrow Malay nationalism, or more correctly racialism, began to spread, especially amongst the younger Malays. They invariably blamed the Chinese for their poverty and lack of opportunities in business. Thus feelings against the Chinese began to mount again. Issues such as the national language, Chinese schools, the continued dominance of English schools, and the failure of the few Malay enterprises, began to be played up.

While the English language press was still under British management and took a very liberal stance with regard to the problems, frequently being unsympathetic in its attitude towards the Malays, the various vernacular newspapers belonging to each ethnic community were far from reluctant to stir up racial issues. The Government did nothing to try to curb the communally biased and inflammatory reporting. Indeed Tunku Abdul Rahman, the prime minister, and the other leaders of the Alliance Government appeared quite sanguine, believing that the absence of open clashes between the Malays and the Chinese reflected underlying racial harmony in the country. But on the ground tension between the two races was mounting.

Matters came to a head in 1969. The general election of that year was unique because the Alliance Government was so confident of winning that it decided to allow the campaign to run the full length of time allowed under the constitution. During the six weeks of campaigning, tension mounted as each party tried to rally support by appealing openly to racial sentiments. It must also be borne in mind that, in 1969, the communist insurgents, mainly Chinese, were still very active against government forces in the jungles of Peninsular Malaysia and also in the East Malaysian state of Sarawak. This served to heighten the tension.

UMNO found itself losing support to the more racialist PMIP, while the MCA was battered by the other Chinese-based parties for not being more Chinese. Communist sympathisers fanned the flames of racial hatred. In Penang an UMNO party worker was killed, and in Kuala Lumpur a blatantly communist sympathiser also lost his life. The funeral for the latter was held during the campaign period, and was exploited to rouse Chinese racial and communist sentiments.

The Alliance still won the parliamentary elections, albeit with a reduced majority. But at state level the Alliance fared far worse. It failed to recapture Kelantan from PMIP, lost Penang to the newly formed and Chinese-based Gerakan party, and was unable to form governments in Perak and Selangor, where it failed to win a clear majority of seats.

The poor performance of the Alliance was treated by the opposition as a kind of victory for them. The Chinese opposition parties went further and celebrated what they blatantly declared was a Chinese victory over the Malays. The final straw came when they were given permission to hold a victory parade in Kuala Lumpur, during which they deliberately taunted the Malays. Suddenly, racial clashes erupted, people were killed and property was set on fire.

Prompt action by the Government stopped the riots from spreading throughout the country. The situation in Kuala Lumpur was quickly restored to an uneasy calm. But the Government leaders were no longer confident of reuniting the different races. Indeed, during the height of the rioting, one senior Malay leader declared that democracy was dead in Malaysia. Foreign observers gleefully pointed out that their dire predictions about Malaysia had been correct. They had always said that Malaysia would go up in flames as the incompatible races clashed, and the race riots of May 1969 clearly showed they were right.

Today, a quarter of a century later, Malaysia is not only peaceful and politically stable, but also prosperous, having grown at a rate averaging over 7% per annum since 1970. The different races seem to be getting on well together. Indeed the enlarged coalition of racially based parties, Barisan Nasional (BN) or the National Front, the successor to the Alliance, which forms the central government and most of the state governments, is stronger than ever. In business, partnership between the different races is common and remarkably successful. Malays, Chinese and Indians work in each other's companies, not only at the lower levels, but as executives as well. There is still consciousness of ethnic identities, but the prejudices have diminished considerably.

The situation in Malaysia today is radically different from that in 1969 and before. Not only is there no palpable racial tension, but Malaysia is now recognised as one of the very few countries where a multiracial people have been able to build a prosperous nation, through their tolerance and cooperation with one another. In fact, Malaysia is mentioned more and more as a model of racial harmony and cooperation in a multiracial society.

FORMULATING THE NEW ECONOMIC POLICY

The economic disparities which characterised the early years of independence have also visibly diminished. They have not been totally eradicated, but they are no longer so obvious. There may have been other causes for the racial tensions of the 1950s and 1960s, but at least those that could be attributed to the disparities in the distribution of the national wealth have been much reduced.

How has this come about? The race riots of 1969 clearly awoke the leaders of the Alliance Government and some of the opposition to the fact that the economic imbalances between the races were an important contributory factor to poor race relations. They reasoned that, although the ethnic, language and cultural differences could not be changed or removed, the economic disparities could be.

The interim National Operations Council, set up following the riots of 1969, closely examined the root causes of the economic disparities, and the unequal development of the indigenous and the non-indigenous people. Their findings confirmed what everyone had suspected all along. Poverty was high amongst the *bumiputeras* or the indigenous people, predominantly Malays, while the remainder were mainly in the lower income category. The *bumiputeras* were also largely employed in the agricultural sector.

A National Consultative Council, with representatives drawn from all the major races, was set up to help formulate a new economic policy to restructure the economy, so that a more equitable distribution of wealth could be achieved between the races. Obviously, the emphasis would be on bringing the *bumiputeras* into the mainstream of the economic life of the nation. The idea was to enrich them without impoverishing the other races by expropriating their wealth. It was to be a process of levelling up rather than levelling down.

Accordingly, the twin objectives of the New Economic Policy

(NEP), launched at the start of 1971 and planned to cover the next twenty years, were:
• the eradication of poverty irrespective of race;
• the elimination of the identification of race with economic function.

In 1969 Malaysia was still largely an agricultural country. Business was limited to tin mining, rubber planting and the importation, distribution and retailing of essential goods and a few luxury items. There was hardly any manufacturing industry and the service sector was quite rudimentary. The utilities were owned and operated by the Government. They practically never brought in any revenue for the state, and in many instances had to be subsidised from public funds. But they provided employment for quite a large number of people, mostly *bumiputeras*. In those days of high unemployment, this was important.

Wealth has historically been related to the ownership of land, and the early attempts to create wealth amongst the Malays were through land settlements. Unfortunately, the limited availability of land restricted this approach. In any case, the ownership of small agricultural landholdings would never have given the *bumiputeras* the wealth to balance that of the other races.

Moving the *bumiputeras* into the mainstream of economic activity was easier said than done. The Malays were unskilled in business and the use of money. They did not regard money as capital. Money to the rural Malays in particular was simply a convenience used for acquiring needed goods. The educational level of the *bumiputeras* was also very low. There were few university graduates and still fewer qualified professionals. Of the total registered professionals in 1970, only 4.9% were *bumiputeras*.

At that time, the banking system in Malaysia was not concerned with supporting social and economic objectives. The banks were purely money-lending institutions and did not see any role for themselves in the restructuring of society. With the exception of Bank Bumiputera, which was set up to help the *bumiputeras* gain access to capital, the banks did not consider it an obligation to make loans available to aspiring *bumiputera* businessmen. MARA, the misnamed Majlis Amanah Rakyat or Council of Trust for the People, and successor to the Rural Industrial Development Authority, focused only on small businesses and was not yet an effective agency for projecting the *bumiputeras* into the mainstream of business life.

While the objectives of the NEP were clear, the methods and approaches required to achieve them were not so obvious. There was at that time no real model anywhere in the world for the Malaysian Government to follow. The affirmative action policy was not yet conceived in the USA. Consequently, the Barisan Nasional Government had to muddle through, making quite a number of costly mistakes along the way.

RESTRUCTURING FOR EQUITY AND JUSTICE

Social restructuring for equity and justice was not new. Many western ideologists and revolutionaries had tried to restructure their societies, in order to overcome perceived injustices and inequalities. Thus the communist and socialist ideologies were formulated in the late 19th century by Karl Marx, Friedrich Engels and others, because these western thinkers felt that the societies in which they lived were unjust due to the exploitation of the workers by the rich capitalists. The latter used their capital to amass huge fortunes, while the workers were paid wages which could hardly sustain a decent and tolerable life.

In the course of the 19th century, the industrial revolution fundamentally changed most parts of western Europe. Feudal agrarian society, dating from the Middle Ages, was replaced by a society polarised between the rich capitalist few and the poor masses or workers. The western thinkers assumed that, if the state owned and controlled all industries and all agricultural land, or 'the means of production' as they termed them, all the profits would accrue to the state, which would distribute them equitably to the workers. In the pursuit of this Marxist ideal, communists violently expropriated the property of the capitalists, while socialists preferred a less radical mixture of nationalisation and punitive taxes on the wealthy.

The Malaysian Government was never attracted to either communism or socialism, and models such as the Soviet Union or post-war Britain were not considered suitable for the purpose of restructuring Malaysian society, in order to eradicate poverty and remove the identification of race with economic function. The Malaysian Government therefore had to formulate its own methods. Quite obviously, it would not be able to come up with perfect solutions. Mistakes were made which attracted much criticism from all and sundry. But the Government persisted in devising new policies and initiatives, in order to bring about the success of the NEP.

If the *bumiputeras* were to play a more equitable role in the economy, they had to be equipped not just with capital and opportunities, but also with the necessary education and know-how. Providing the required level of education and training takes time, while the NEP was given only twenty years to achieve a specific set of targets, involving a redistribution of the economic cake. The aim was to increase the share held by the *bumiputeras* from 2.4% to 30%, although they constituted 56% of the population, while at the same time increasing the non-*bumiputera* share from 34.3% to 40%, and reducing the share held by foreigners from 63.3% to 30%.

If these targets were to be achieved in twenty years, the *bumiputeras* would have to move into business, even big business, very quickly. Positive discrimination or, as the Americans termed it when trying to help the blacks and Hispanics, affirmative action had to be implemented immediately. Government contracts, licences and special considerations were given to *bumiputeras* trying to gatecrash into various economic activities, previously monopolised by the Chinese or foreigners.

While a few *bumiputeras* were quite successful, many failed or abused the policy. It was at this time that the term 'Ali Baba' was coined to describe a common form of NEP abuse. Many Malays lent their names to so-called joint ventures, in which they were quite literally sleeping partners. Many of them became rich through the contracts and licences given to them simply because they were *bumiputeras*, but which they promptly sold to their so-called 'Ali Baba' joint venture partners or other non-*bumiputeras*.

Unfortunately, attention was focused exclusively on these *bumiputeras* who abused the NEP and became fleetingly wealthy as a result. The NEP was not just about giving *bumiputeras* business opportunities through contracts and exclusive licences, in order that they could enrich themselves quickly. The main thrust of the NEP was to prepare the *bumiputeras*, through education and training, to enter lucrative economic activities and employment on a permanent and successful basis.

This was never going to be easy. The *bumiputeras* were historically a farming, petty trading and civil service community, who had a lackadaisical, even naive, attitude towards money and business. A cultural reformation, involving new skills, new approaches and new values, was essential if the *bumiputeras* were going to be changed into a confident, commercially sophisticated community, capable of competing with the non-*bumiputera* business community. Without this cultural change the *bumiputeras* would fail, and, if they failed, the NEP would fail too.

Education and training therefore made up the biggest element in the NEP's initiatives. Where once only members of the ruling houses and the sons of senior Malay officials were able to obtain a good education, under the NEP a major drive was mounted to give less privileged Malays and other *bumiputeras*, particularly those living in the rural areas, access to education and training at all levels. Schools, including good secondary and residential schools, were built and staffed with qualified teachers, in order to bring a high standard of education to all *bumiputeras*, be they urban or rural.

Scholarships for secondary schools and universities, both at home and abroad, were greatly increased. MARA took the lead by building Sekolah Menengah Rendah Sains Mara, or Junior Science Colleges, to cater for the brighter *bumiputera* students, and by handing out full scholarships for the study of numerous disciplines locally and overseas. The stress was not only on academic subjects, but also on non-academic qualifications. Thus many Malays qualified as tailors and cutters, after being trained in these skills by experts in England. Many *bumiputeras* obtained an MBA (Master in Business Administration) from well-known universities, and large numbers attended business management courses. Numerous training centres were set up in Malaysia to produce mechanics, craftsmen and other skilled workers. *Bumiputera* youths were also sent to learn various crafts, such as woodcarving, in neighbouring countries. These students and trainees were the main beneficiaries of the NEP. Later, many went into business, including big business, and prospered. No one could fail to see the benefits that the NEP brought to all *bumiputeras*, with some perhaps gaining more than others.

However, the initial attempt to break into the world of big business through individual efforts attracted considerable attention and many adverse comments, as the contribution of such direct participation by individuals to the NEP targets was at first very small. In near desperation, the Government decided to set up state-owned companies to enter areas of business where the *bumiputeras* lacked capital, opportunities or expertise. All the state governments were instructed to set up State Economic Development Corporations (SEDCs). These corporations in turn set up companies, which were given *bumiputera* status and were involved in a variety of businesses. State resources such as timber and minerals were allocated to these companies for exploitation. While the SEDCs succeeded in increasing the *bumiputera* share of the national wealth, they often failed to operate profitably. At the same time, they frequently found themselves competing not only with non-*bumiputera* businessmen, but also with the handful of capable individual *bumiputeras* keen to get involved in these business fields.

With a few exceptions, the SEDCs were unable to contribute much towards the objectives of the NEP. By 1985, 206 companies had been set up by the SEDCs, with a total paid-up capital of RM1,273 million. Over half of these companies (57.2% of the total) did not make any profit. By 1990 the number of companies had increased to 258, with a paid-up capital of RM2,126 million. Fortunately, the number of loss-making companies had declined, mainly due to the economic recovery in the late 1980s. However, there were still several SEDCs, including those from Pahang and Negeri Sembilan, which had a high percentage of unprofitable companies.

Meanwhile, the Federal Government was pursuing a similar business strategy to the SEDCs. By 1985, 392 companies had been set up under the Federal Government, with a total paid-up capital of RM10,099 million. This number had increased to 462 companies by 1990, with a paid-up capital of RM18,860. Unfortunately, their performance was not much better than that of the SEDC companies.

Despite the NEP bias in favour of the *bumiputeras*, the Malaysian economy was expanding. New enterprises were being set up by the non-*bumiputeras*, especially the Chinese, while foreign businesses and investment were also expanding. Since no expropriation of existing assets of the non-*bumiputeras* was allowed under the NEP, it was left to the expanding economic cake as a whole to contribute towards the redistribution of wealth. It was therefore necessary for the *bumiputeras* to be allocated at least 30% of the shares issued whenever a company expanded, or a new company was started or listed on the Kuala Lumpur Stock Exchange (KLSE).

Initially, the shares were allocated to *bumiputera* individuals who applied to buy them. Sold at par value to the *bumiputeras*, these shares naturally commanded a much higher market price, and many of the *bumiputeras* resold them to make a quick profit. Matters worsened when, in some cases, *bumiputeras* were actually financed by non-*bumiputeras* who wanted to buy the shares themselves, in many instances also reselling them for a quick profit. This scam benefited only a small number of *bumiputeras*, and even then only temporarily, as they frittered away their new-found wealth. The *bumiputera* share of ownership in economic enterprises did not increase in the long run. Indeed, the reverse happened. Non-*bumiputera* ownership was enhanced.

Accordingly, it was decided that the biggest portion of the shares allocated to the *bumiputeras* should be given to the Government companies representing the *bumiputeras*. Unfortunately, this resulted in genuine *bumiputera* investors being deprived of the chance to invest in profitable companies. At the same time, since the state-owned companies were usually represented only on the boards of directors of the enterprises concerned and were on the whole thinly spread, their contribution to the management of these enterprises was minimal. In other words, such participation did not result in the *bumiputeras* acquiring business and entrepreneurial skills. The benefits to the *bumiputeras* and the contribution to the success of the NEP were therefore negligible. The only positive result that followed from the shares being allocated to state-owned companies was to increase considerably the stake of the *bumiputeras* in business.

By and large, the *bumiputeras* were dissatisfied with the Government companies holding their shares in trust. The percentage of *bumiputera* holdings had gone up, but the wealth accruing to *bumiputeras* as individuals was minimal. The dissatisfaction of the *bumiputeras* was amplified by the Government's tendency to favour state-owned companies in the allocation of contracts for construction or supplies. In many instances, these companies were monopolistic and obstructed the entry of private sector *bumiputera* enterprises into the business concerned.

In 1977, in an effort to distribute the shares to individual *bumiputeras*, while preventing them from passing into the hands of non-*bumiputeras*, the Government struck upon the idea of unit trusts. Permodalan Nasional Berhad (PNB), or the National Equity Corporation, was set up in March 1978, and the Government allocated the new body a capital sum of RM3 billion. The money was used for the purchase of a *bumiputera* 30% share stake in companies that were either expanding their capital base or newly listed on the KLSE. The PNB was additionally tasked with purchasing shares in blue-chip companies on the KLSE at market price, and could also buy up well-run companies through the local or foreign bourses. The portfolio of companies was put into an open-ended unit trust, the Amanah Saham Nasional (ASN), or National Unit Trust, and shares were sold as units to the *bumiputeras*. The price of the ASN shares was fixed at RM1. The managers undertook to buy back the shares at a fixed discount. Sales other than to the managers were not permitted.

In order to make the unit trust attractive, the dividends paid out were always higher than the current fixed-deposit rates. Indeed, the margin between interest rates and dividends was always kept fairly high, so much so that the banks were actually prepared to lend money for the purpose of purchasing the ASN shares. The high return was possible because the Malaysian economy was strong and most companies performed well.

Various gimmicks were used to attract *bumiputera* investors to purchase shares in the ASN. For an investment of only RM10, one hundred of the RM1 units could be bought. The rest would be paid from the yearly dividends. Since such dividends usually exceeded 12% per annum, in less than nine years the *bumiputera* investor would have paid off the sum owed for the one hundred units. Major publicity campaigns were mounted in order to explain the workings of the unit trust and the dividends paid, as compared to other forms of savings. In the process, the *bumi-*

puteras gained a better understanding of the workings of the stock market. Later they were able to participate more fully by investing on the KLSE themselves.

To ensure that the richer *bumiputeras* did not take advantage of the high returns from the unit trust, a limit of 50,000 units was put on the purchase each individual could make. Clearly, the main beneficiaries of the unit trust would be the poorer *bumiputera* investors. For the richer ones, the limit was too low to benefit them substantially.

The success of the ASN and later the Amanah Saham Bumiputera (ASB), or Bumiputera Unit Trust, in distributing wealth to the *bumiputeras* has been phenomenal. By the end of 1990, nearly 2.5 million *bumiputera* individuals had invested in the ASN, while almost 2.6 million individuals had invested in the ASB. The investments were admittedly not big, but, through the PNB, *bumiputera* participation in the economy has become much more widespread and equitable. This belies the accusation that the NEP benefited only a few privileged *bumiputeras*. Of course, unit trust investors do not become rich, but there is no society in which everyone is rich. The non-*bumiputeras* are not all rich. What the unit trusts have done is enable a greater number of people to have a share in the nation's prosperity, and to raise their incomes a little. The objective of the NEP was never to enrich all the *bumiputeras*, so that they actually became better off than the non-*bumiputera* communities. The NEP was not about reversing the distribution of wealth between the races. It aimed at achieving an equitable distribution at all levels between the different communities. There had to be proportionately the same percentages of rich and poor *bumiputeras* as there were rich and poor non-*bumiputeras*.

The unit trusts, as operated by the PNB, were by far the best method of achieving an equitable distribution of shares and dividends amongst the largest possible number of *bumiputeras*, resulting from the restructuring of companies under the NEP. Unfortunately, the shareholders could not participate actively in the businesses in which they had indirectly invested. Except for a small number of *bumiputeras*, who were involved in the management of the unit trusts and in investing for the trusts on the stock markets, direct *bumiputera* participation in business was still far less than that of the non-*bumiputeras*.

If the NEP was to be truly meaningful, there had to be adequate direct *bumiputera* participation in all areas of business, from manufacturing to wholesaling, retailing and marketing. There had to be as many *bumiputera* small businesses and big businesses as the proportion allocated to them, i.e. 30%. Finally, there had to be a proportionate number of *bumiputera* executives and non-executives at all levels.

A *BUMIPUTERA* COMMERCIAL COMMUNITY

By the mid-1980s, a few *bumiputeras* had emerged who seemed able to manage business enterprises effectively and profitably. Some had progressed on their own, while others had worked for *bumiputera*-owned or state-owned companies. Indeed, some had worked in non-*bumiputera* and foreign-owned companies which subscribed to the objectives of the NEP. In the banking sector, the managers and top executives of state-owned banks or banks in which the Government had substantial shareholdings were mostly *bumiputeras*. They had shown that they were competent in the world of banking and finance.

Meanwhile, the Government's educational drive had produced a better educated corps of *bumiputera* professionals, some of whom had undertaken training in business management. A number of Harvard and Wharton business school graduates were to be found amongst the senior Government executives and in the big non-*bumiputera* firms, where they filled posts with genuine responsibility, rather than merely being appointed as figureheads.

Institut Teknologi Mara and the Malaysian universities, which included Universiti Utara Malaysia, an institution dedicated exclusively to management training, had also enlarged the pool of trained and competent *bumiputera* management graduates. Many of the companies which the PNB controlled or owned, a substantial number of them quite large enterprises, had been fairly well managed by their newly qualified *bumiputera* managers, yielding good profits.

Clearly, in the latter years of the NEP a body of able *bumiputera* business executives had been built up. Some of them had enough confidence to resign as executives of well-known companies, in order to go into business on their own. They began to recognise the opportunities available under the NEP, and they took them up as challenges. These new entrepreneurs were a different breed of people. They were not the kind thrown up in the early years of the NEP, whose main intention had been to lend their names to the 'Ali Baba' type of joint ventures. The new entrepreneurs were self-confident and able, and tended to own and manage their business enterprises themselves. Their principal areas of involvement were telecommunications, finance and manufacturing.

It is true that some still depended on the favour shown by the Government to *bumiputeras* under the NEP. They were able to win contracts, and acquire licences and permits, which placed them in a favourable position to go into certain businesses. However, it must be pointed out that the non-*bumiputeras* were not really deprived, as certain Government contracts were beyond the capacity of *bumiputera*-owned or even state-owned enterprises. Despite the NEP, a large number of Government contracts and almost all contracts in the private sector went to non-*bumiputera* companies. The accusation that the NEP deprived the non-*bumiputeras* of business opportunities is therefore without basis.

The abilities of the *bumiputeras* and their companies slowly came to be recognised. As a result of the rapid expansion of the telecommunications infrastructure planned by the Department of Telecommunications, cable-laying contracts were farmed out to newly formed companies, mostly owned by engineers who had themselves formerly worked for the Department. They had left public service in order to try their luck at running their own contracting companies. The contracts were big, but the capital needed was small enough for these new *bumiputera* entrepreneurs to raise it. Most were borrowed from the banks, which regarded the contracts as good guarantees. The banks were not really taking any serious risks, being quite certain that, if these *bumiputera* contractors failed, the contracts would go to experienced non-*bumiputera* companies able to complete the projects. Out of these contracts emerged some of the strongest *bumiputera*-owned and managed contracting companies, which later went into manufacturing, construction in other fields, trading and the development of hotels and resorts.

One of the most prolific producers of able *bumiputera* managers and entrepreneurs was the Urban Development Authority (UDA) and its subsidiary, Peremba, which were largely involved in property development. These individuals later went on to manage big *bumiputera* firms. Subsequently, they set up and managed their own businesses, which became involved in diverse industries.

The emergence of these able and capable *bumiputera* businessmen, executives and entrepreneurs was crucial to the next stage of the NEP. Admittedly, this stage was not initially planned. It was a case of the Government seizing an opportunity which had presented itself.

In the mid-1980s the Malaysian economy was not doing very well. The country was experiencing a recession and the Government was unable to generate enough funds to support high levels of economic growth. Yet the NEP was dependent on an expanding economy and the distribution of new wealth in favour of the *bumiputeras*. Not only would a recession severely curb this distribution of wealth, but it might also arouse considerable resentment amongst the non-*bumiputeras*.

The Government adopted several measures to stimulate the economy, aimed initially at job creation. By 1984–5 *bumiputera* scholarship holders, who had qualified in various professions, were returning home to find no jobs waiting for them. They were unemployed and becoming more embittered with each passing day. To overcome this problem, the Government had to put them into sinecure jobs, paying them a paltry RM400 a month. Private firms were urged to employ them, and to pay this very small salary. Unemployment amongst skilled and unskilled workers was also high. The economy was stagnating. The business climate was generally depressing and Government revenue was no longer growing. Indeed, it was shrinking. Progress in the implementation of the NEP had ground almost to a halt.

CHANGES OF STRATEGY

To stimulate investment in industries which would create jobs, the Government had to hold in abeyance certain aspects of the NEP. The ownership of new enterprises by *bumiputeras* had to be sacrificed in favour of creating employment for them. In other words, the interests of *bumiputera* investors and entrepreneurs had to be sacrificed in favour of *bumiputera* workers, and indeed those of other races. Here is another instance where the NEP favoured the ordinary *bumiputera*, rather than the few rich *bumiputeras* whom the policy has been said to have benefited exclusively.

Foreign investment was encouraged through the removal of many of the restrictions on full ownership. Provided the industries set up were export oriented, or alternatively employed a large number of workers, foreign investors were allowed total ownership. Equity participation by *bumiputeras* or other Malaysians was not necessary, but was instead left to the discretion of the investors concerned.

Almost immediately investments began to flow in. New jobs were created, helping to reduce unemployment. This policy has been so successful that today Malaysia is actually short of workers. Some 2 million foreign workers have moved in to take up the numerous job opportunities created. Practically no other developing country, or developed country for that matter, has been able to achieve this level of success in recent years, and all this despite the NEP. The shortage is now not only amongst blue-collar workers, but has spread to engineers and other professionals. Wages have gone up, and trained professionals and skilled workers are actually able to demand the salary they want when applying for jobs.

The economy was clearly growing again, indeed, growing with a vengeance. By 1987, just one year after the NEP was less rigorously enforced, the turnaround in the Malaysian economy had become obvious. Employment had reached record levels. Consequently, the problems faced by the Government were no longer those of failure, but the more 'pleasant' ones of success.

One of the major problems faced by the Government was, and still is, that of providing adequate infrastructure for a rapidly expanding economy. Roads, airports, ports, power generation, telecommunications and the water supply all had to keep pace with the demands of business and the nation as a whole. It was also clear that the increase in living standards in Malaysia had raised expectations amongst the people. The old roads, telephone service and power supply were not up to the standard expected by the new, more affluent Malaysian consumers and users. They expected facilities to be of the same, or nearly the same, standard as those in the developed countries of the West.

The Government found itself unable to cope with these rising demands. Revenue was not growing fast enough and Government borrowing had reached the limits that it had legally permitted itself, despite several upward revisions. It had no choice but to give out more and more contracts to the private sector. Even then the Government was unable to supervise or monitor effectively the implementation of these projects, as it was very short-staffed.

The Government had earlier announced that it was going to privatise some of the state-owned companies. From the outset, privatisation faced many constraints. The Government could not abandon the NEP, so somehow privatisation had to be made to comply with the NEP objectives, if this new strategy was not going to attract adverse political reaction from the *bumiputeras*.

Privatisation had not been very successful in many other countries. There was much opposition to it, especially from the employees, who saw the downsizing for efficiency which invariably accompanied privatisation, as a threat to their jobs. They were not going to sacrifice themselves for the sake of efficiency and the profitability of the newly privatised entities. There were no good models for the Malaysian Government to follow. Certainly, there was no model where privatisation had also to serve social and ethnic restructuring objectives.

After the announcement of the Government's intention to privatise, there was much discussion and numerous studies were undertaken in order to reduce opposition to the policy, and ensure its success. The opposition of the workers was to be overcome by guaranteeing that there would be no lay-offs, and that their wages and perks would be no less than they had received in public service. Indeed, they were to be allowed to remain on the Government pay scales, with subsequent revisions, if they wished, although the wages offered by the company on privatisation were guaranteed to be higher than those paid by the Government. In addition, so as to make privatisation even more attractive, employees choosing to be paid under the privatised wage scheme would be eligible to purchase a certain percentage of the company's shares, upon privatisation, at the offer price. Should a bonus be declared, only those on the privatised scheme would be eligible. The Government had never paid bonuses before, and was not about to start now.

There was still scepticism and a reluctance on the part of the employees until the first big privatisation project, the Department of Telecommunications, which became Telekom Malaysia, proved a resounding success. The incomes of the employees who had opted for Telekom Malaysia's new pay scheme were much higher than the wages and perks they had received while the service was operated by the Government.

Complying with the NEP requirement for *bumiputera* participation proved less difficult than expected. By the time the privatisation policy was implemented, a significant number of *bumiputera* companies, entrepreneurs and managers had emerged. This enabled the Government to sell the state-owned entities to thriving *bumiputera*-owned or controlled firms. Almost from nowhere, genuine and highly skilled *bumiputera* entrepreneurs emerged to accept the challenge of buying and operating the privatised entities. The early success of Telekom Malaysia and Projek Lebuhraya Utara Selatan (PLUS), the builder and operator of the North–South Highway, convinced the Government that privatisation would not only be a solution to the shortage of public funds for infrastructure development, but also contribute towards the objectives of the NEP. This was because the *bumiputera* companies were able to take up all, or nearly all, of the share allocation of the privatised entities, thus making a bigger contribution to the NEP targets than if they were allocated a mere 30% stake, with little role to play in the management of the newly privatised concerns. A number of these *bumiputera*-owned and managed companies were later listed on the KLSE, making their shares available to non-*bumiputeras*, but this did not pose a problem to the achievement of the NEP targets. *Bumiputeras* had developed the capacity to buy substantial shares in non-*bumiputera* companies, or even to take them over completely, so that the sale of shares in *bumiputera* companies was balanced by their purchases.

The restructuring of newly listed and expanding non-*bumiputera* companies had to go on in accordance with the guidelines of the NEP, because, despite privatisation, the rapidly growing economy demanded much higher investments by the *bumiputeras* in order to achieve the 30% stake allocated to them. There was little need for sacrifice on the part of the non-*bumiputeras*, because their share had expanded beyond the 40% stake allocated to them under the NEP, due to the ownership of many of the big foreign firms having fallen into their hands.

It is necessary at this point to be reminded of one of the twin objectives of the NEP: the elimination of the identification of race with economic function. To be really meaningful, all races had to be represented at all levels of the economy. In other words, not only have there to be *bumiputeras* in business in general, but they had to be more or less proportionately represented at all levels of all kinds of business. There had to be *bumiputeras* in the retail business as there were non-*bumiputeras* in this sector. There had to be *bumiputeras* in the wholesale business and there had to be *bumiputeras* in big business too. Only then would the wealth distribution between *bumiputeras* and non-*bumiputeras* be seen to be equitable. Only then would there truly be no identification of race with economic function.

PRIVATISATION AS A STRATEGIC APPROACH

Privatisation presented an opportunity to create *bumiputera*-owned businesses of the same scale and level as the most successful non-*bumiputera* industrial and commercial giants, which were fast evolving into huge conglomerates.

At the beginning of the NEP, most non-*bumiputera* companies were family owned and were relatively small and unsophisticated. Family companies almost invariably break up on the demise of the founder. The sons and daughters who inherit these enterprises often cannot get along, and they tend to go their separate ways with their individual portions of the inheritance. For as long as the non-*bumiputeras* conducted business through family companies, these concerns could not be large in scale, nor could they be perpetuated over generations. Consequently, there were no non-*bumiputera* corporations of the calibre and age of foreign-owned companies, such as Sime Darby, Guthrie, Barlow and Boustead.

In the 1980s this situation changed as the Chinese family concerns began to give way to Chinese-controlled public limited companies. The role of the founder entrepreneur remained, but the capacity for the enterprises to grow very big and to spawn new and equally powerful public limited companies improved greatly. Non-*bumiputera* conglomerates involved in a wide spectrum of businesses began to emerge. These conglomerates were growing bigger and bigger, and looked likely to become household names, even on a global scale. This posed a new challenge to the NEP. If the identification of race with economic function was to be eliminated, there had to be big *bumiputera*-dominated, public limited companies involved in a variety of manufacturing, trading and service activities, and capable of surviving beyond the original founder.

When the Government decided to privatise certain state-owned entities, the opportunity was taken to help a number of fairly successful *bumiputeras* move directly into big business. One of the best examples of this was the privatisation of the North–South Highway. Roads in Malaysia had always been the responsibility of the Government. There was some logic in this. Since the Government collected taxes, including various revenues from motor vehicles, it was only right that the Government should build and maintain the roads. However, the capacity of the Government to build modern highways was limited by the revenues received. Even if the highways were tolled, the earnings were usually insufficient to maintain them, much less build new ones. In any case, the Government had never been good at managing commercial enterprises, as had been demonstrated by the losses incurred by state-owned companies.

If the North–South Highway was sold to the private sector at a price which reflected the actual cost of land, construction and other associated expenses, the financial return to the private operator after completing the building works would be negative, even if high toll rates were charged. To be profitable, the Government had to transfer the assets to the private sector at well below cost and, if necessary, subsidise the expense of construction on the unfinished sections.

This sounds like a bad deal for the Government and the people. Why should the Government underprice the North–South Highway and subsidise the project further, to induce the private sector to become involved? The fact was that the Government was getting no return from the Highway anyway. Indeed, the Government was losing money and, in addition, faced the prospect of spending more money to complete the project. When it was finished the losses would have been even greater. Meanwhile, the Government had to build and maintain many secondary roads, which were no less essential to the people. These roads could not be tolled.

If the North–South Highway was transferred to the private sector at nominal cost, Government funds would no longer be needed to complete the project. If loans were given to the private company, they would be repaid in time. If the company earned a profit after completing and operating the toll-road, the Government would gain from corporate taxes. The public would be the biggest beneficiary. The low cost of acquiring the Government assets would enable the private sector operator to keep the toll rates low. In other words, the Government would be subsidising not only the company, but also the public, by helping to keep the tolls low. This was only right because the Government would still be collecting taxes on vehicles and fuel. By helping to keep the tolls low, the Government would be fulfilling its duty to road-users. The state-owned secondary roads which feed the toll roads would remain free.

The most important factor to stress is that privatisation of the

North–South Highway became feasible through this approach by the Government. The private sector of course contributed through good management, not only in operating the toll-road, but also in completing a world-class major highway.

The transfer of the North–South Highway to *bumiputera* entrepreneurs was a great success. It suddenly enabled a *bumiputera* company to leap-frog into the world of big business. From there, the company moved into other businesses where it appears to have been equally successful. Following the success of the North–South Highway, privatisation became the route for projecting *bumiputeras* into this rarefied world.

Such was the performance of these *bumiputera*-owned and managed companies that the Government felt they should also take over the shares of the *bumiputera* unit trusts in companies where *bumiputera* participation was rather indirect and minimal. It is true that the unit trusts enabled more *bumiputeras* to own shares, albeit indirectly, in the big corporations. But these companies were not doing as well as they could, as the shareholders were usually passive and not in any position to stimulate growth in the companies. The benefits to the *bumiputeras* were minimal.

Bumiputera entrepreneurs who had shown good track records in managing and expanding their own organisations were thought capable of improving the performance of these companies, if they were given a substantial personal stake in them. The unit trusts could still retain a reasonable portion of the shares, while the proceeds from the sale of the shares could be invested in other companies. If the companies sold to the *bumiputera* entrepreneurs performed well, the return on the remaining shares held by the unit trusts could be quite substantial, thus giving a better return to the unit trust holders.

This strategy has so far worked very well. The companies which have been sold off to the *bumiputeras* have not only given better returns, but also been more innovatively managed, and have expanded accordingly. In the process, a number of leading *bumiputera* businessmen have emerged and are running conglomerates which are comparable to the large non-*bumiputera* corporations. Thus another aspect of the elimination of the identification of race with economic function has been achieved.

However, this approach is quite risky. The *bumiputera* candidates must be well selected. Their track records must be carefully examined and evaluated. Their experience and the time they have been in business must be such as to reflect true ability and seriousness of purpose. They must not be the kind of people who would sell their shares for quick gains. They must not be 'Ali Babas'!

This is not the kind of opportunity to be given on the basis of favouritism, or to enrich a 'crony' as has often been suggested. The stakes are too high, in terms of both the Government's objectives and its credibility. A majority of the *bumiputeras* who come forward with proposals, for the purchase of shares or companies belonging to the unit trusts or to the Government, do not get their proposals approved. Their unhappiness and criticism of the Government are understandable. At the risk of being accused of favouritism, the Government will continue to be highly selective. More *bumiputeras* will get their chance, but certainly not all or even the majority.

CHANGE IN PERCEPTION

The initial lack of faith in the *bumiputeras* has now almost disappeared. Their enterprises have grown and prospered. They are no longer dependent on Government contracts and projects, although these are still necessary for some of the newer concerns. The *bumiputera* entrepreneurs have gained enough confidence and credibility to encounter little or no difficulty in raising large loans, in order to finance the purchase of the majority of the shares or a controlling interest in the privatised companies. Such is their credibility and capability that they have now ventured abroad to buy and operate businesses in other countries, without the benefit of special support from the Government. At home the big *bumiputera* companies and entrepreneurs have been able to buy into, and actually acquire, major non-*bumiputera* companies. Frequently, they retain the non-*bumiputera* names.

The picture today is very different from that in 1970 and earlier. The imbalances in the economic development of the *bumiputeras* and non-*bumiputeras* have not been totally eliminated, but they are certainly not as glaring as before. The NEP objectives, in terms of wealth redistribution and restructuring to eliminate the identification of race with economic function, have not yet been fully met, but no race can now be said to be unrepresented in any field.

Economic restructuring, as has been pointed out earlier, was not a new thing. The communist and socialist ideologies were formulated in order to correct the perceived imbalance in their societies: the extreme disparity in the distribution of wealth between the rich capitalist owners and the poorly paid workers, whose work resulted in the high profits made by the owners. Although in the capitalist economies the companies were largely publicly listed and shares were sold through the local stock exchange, the workers were usually far too poor to be able to buy them. Consequently, the rich kept getting richer, while the poor kept getting poorer.

Many so-called great western thinkers and ideologists, from Marx and Engels onwards, reasoned that, if the government owned 'the means of production', all the profits would accrue to the state. If the government was representative of the workers, in fact run by the workers through their own political parties or trade unions, the profits would be disbursed more equitably in the form of wages, benefits and subsidies to all the workers and their families. For society to be equitable and just, all the people would have to benefit equally, i.e. wages and benefits would have to be the same for everybody. The end result of this restructuring of the economy would be not only the elimination of the disparities in the ownership and distribution of wealth in society, but that everyone would be equally 'rich'.

These western thinkers had forgotten about human nature. They thought that everyone would be 'happy' if they were equal in every way to everyone else. What they failed to appreciate was that, if all wages, benefits and so on were equal, no one would have any incentive to work harder or accept more responsibilities than his 'comrades'. Individual initiatives would be killed completely and a form of stagnation through equality would follow.

Today, we know that communist and socialist attempts at restructuring society have failed. Absolute equality did not create a heaven for the workers. Rather the reverse happened. Human beings can never be equal to each other in every way, and the effect of equalising incomes was to make everyone poor, not rich. It was a process of levelling down, not up.

When people are poor, the nation must also be poor. Government resources can never be substantial if the people are poor. There will be no significant corporate or income taxes to collect. Even if the government decides to distribute to the people the profits of the state-owned industries, normally used to finance other government activities, such as defence, it will still be unable to subsidise all the benefits associated with a rising standard of living. In any case, profits from the state-run industries under a socialist system were never that substantial, because the industries were not run efficiently and the domestic market was composed of poor people with little spending power. The more the government had to allocate the limited earnings from industry to such things as defence and other administrative functions, the less there was for paying wages and subsidising the needs of the people. The net effect was the same. The people were poor, as wages were very low and subsidies were inadequate due to poor government revenues.

The restructuring objective of the NEP was never intended to achieve absolute equality in economic terms for all Malaysians.

The objective was not to make every Malaysian, from whatever racial group, equally wealthy in every way, or for that matter equally poor. There was no intention to eliminate the different income groups found in Malaysian society. The Government accepted that in relative terms there will always be low incomes, middle incomes, high incomes and even super high incomes amongst the people. The disparities should not be too extreme in absolute terms, but disparities there will always be. The NEP accepted this as an unavoidable reality, even a necessity.

Such disparities are not bad in themselves. They act as incentives which motivate individuals to strive to better themselves and acquire more wealth. Even within the same category of workers, there should be differences in earnings, in order to reward those who in one way or another are more able or more productive. There will always be exceptional individuals, whose skills are well above the average. Their numbers can never be very many. If they made up the majority, they would be the average and not the exception. These people, be they entrepreneurs or workers, must be rewarded with higher incomes, but they must also be taxed more, so reducing the disparities as well as lightening the tax burden, if any, of their lower income colleagues. These taxes will pay for the cost of administration and the utilities, as well as subsidies provided by the Government. Without the rich to tax, the poor would have to be satisfied with a low standard of living and no prospect of help from subsidies and publicly funded utilities.

If the above average or the exceptional are amply rewarded, it will never cost society that much as their numbers are always small. But the rewards act as an incentive for them and for others to strive harder. The majority will always earn less than these people, but the competition between workers in the same category, stimulated by incentives, increases efficiency and productivity. This improves the earnings and profits of the company, which in the end benefits all workers, and of course the enterprise as a whole. One way or another, the earnings and the profits will be spent, creating jobs and other businesses, which will again benefit society as a whole.

Similarly, in any society there must be some who are very, very rich. Provided their wealth is legitimately earned, society should never begrudge them their riches. Instead society should utilise their wealth to help the rest of the people, directly through higher taxes on the wealthy, and indirectly through encouraging them to reinvest and to spend their income. Such investments create wealth for others through job creation, and the purchase of goods and services of all kinds. It must always be remembered that one person's expenditure is another person's income. Wealth must eventually be spent and will contribute towards the creation of more wealth in one way or another. A virtuous cycle of growth and wealth creation will be set in motion. The wealth created will be lost to the nation only if it is hoarded or spent outside the country.

CONCLUSION

The NEP, it must be reiterated, was not concerned with making all the *bumiputeras* earn equally, or share equally, the wealth distributed amongst them. This would have made the *bumiputeras* all equally poor, not equally rich. When shares or contracts were given out, they were not distributed equally. In the first place, the amount was never enough to make any difference to the millions of *bumiputeras* who would have been considered eligible purely because they were *bumiputeras*. In the second place, the capacity of every *bumiputera* to acquire the shares was not equal. This would have meant giving them out free, but distributing wealth in such a way would create a dependence mentality, which would only weaken the character of the *bumiputeras*. It has been noted that workers in communist and socialist societies were not generally inclined to work. The NEP was never intended to make the *bumiputeras* lazy. In the third place, the NEP was not merely about distributing wealth amongst the *bumiputeras*, but also to reflect the distribution of wealth amongst the non-*bumiputeras*. Mere wealth without the skill to manage it is not durable. The NEP was about active and meaningful participation in business by *bumiputeras*, so that they could acquire wealth and retain it. Quite obviously, it would be impossible to give every *bumiputera*, some 10 million of them in total, the major controlling interest in all enterprises. By the same token, some *bumiputeras* had to play a greater role and some a lesser role, and the majority very little role, in the management of business enterprises. Their rewards too could never be equal. They had to reflect the roles they played, or the rewards would not be commensurate with the roles.

The intention of the NEP was to create in the *bumiputera* community the same division of labour and rewards as was found in the non-*bumiputera* communities, particularly the Chinese. The *bumiputeras* had to have as big a proportion of low income groups as was found amongst the non-*bumiputeras*, the same proportion of middle income and also of high income. The equitableness was to be not between individuals, but between the communities. This was to be achieved by the elimination of the identification of race with economic function. No longer would the *bumiputeras* be the rural dwellers and peasants. No longer would the non-*bumiputeras* be the urbanites, involved in all kinds of lucrative business activities. The Malays, the Chinese, the Indians, the Ibans, the Kadazans, the Bajaus, the Muruts and so on would be equally represented in the rural and in the urban areas, doing jobs which were no longer specific to any of them.

There remained the question of selection. While there should not be absolute equality within the *bumiputera* community, neither should there be too great a disparity in the distribution of opportunities and wealth as a result of the NEP. However, capabilities had to be taken into consideration. Some *bumi-*

puteras had access to direct wealth acquisition during the early stages of the NEP. They were selected because, one way or another, they managed to convince the authorities that they were capable, whether due to their experience, capital or qualifications. Admittedly, some were also probably selected because of 'connections'. But, as the NEP progressed, the number of *bumiputeras* helped became so large that the idea that connections influenced the choice became quite absurd. The emphasis on education and training, in order to help the upward mobility of the *bumiputeras*, resulted in literally millions of *bumiputeras* benefiting from the NEP.

The tendency to focus only on big successful companies and entrepreneurs is still prevalent, and continues to create the impression that the NEP benefited only a select group of *bumiputeras*. Despite their numbers being quite large, it was assumed that they were favoured because of their connections. A chorus of criticisms from foreign observers was actually echoed by some *bumiputeras* themselves. These *bumiputera* critics, usually highly educated and holding down jobs with good pay, did not pause to think of their own personal situation. They were in fact key beneficiaries of the NEP and the pro-*bumiputera* policies prior to it, having been given scholarships, education and jobs largely because they were *bumiputeras*, and were therefore eligible for discriminatory Government support. Of course, they did not get the opportunities that some other *bumiputeras* were getting in business due to the NEP, but they had already benefited from the NEP through education and employment opportunities. It is unlikely that, if the scholarships and jobs had been competed for by everybody, including the non-*bumiputeras*, they would have been so fortunate in their education or employment. Prior to the pro-*bumiputera* policies, there was actually active discrimination against the *bumiputeras*. If nothing else, the NEP overcame this anti-*bumiputera* discrimination.

The truth is that, under the NEP, all *bumiputeras* were given opportunities according to their capabilities and qualifications.

Where before *bumiputeras* in the rural areas had little access to a secondary education, secondary schools were now built in rural areas to cater for them. Others were given scholarships for residential schools in the urban areas, or for special schools such as the Mara Junior Science Colleges. Those who did well enough were given scholarships to universities and institutions of higher learning at home and abroad. Almost without exception, jobs were waiting for them when they graduated.

Loans, business premises and all sorts of other benefits and opportunities were made available at all levels under the NEP, where before there were none or they were difficult to obtain. Shares from the restructuring of companies were made available to all *bumiputeras* through the unit trusts operated by the PNB. Those who had the means were given opportunities to invest in big business, or to set up their own companies.

There cannot be any *bumiputera* who can honestly say he has not benefited at all from the implementation of the NEP.

As far as the eradication of poverty is concerned, this too has been largely achieved. No one willing to work should face absolute poverty in Malaysia. Even the disabled have been given opportunities to work and earn a living. Those incapable of helping themselves have been assisted through various poverty eradication programmes, including the provision of funds to build or repair their houses. There is truly no reason for poverty to exist, whether in the urban or rural areas, or amongst the *bumiputeras* or the non-*bumiputeras*. Relative poverty is unavoidable, but in Malaysia no one should be so poor in absolute terms that they starve as a result. The fact that some two million foreigners are working in Malaysia is testimony to the extent of opportunities to work and earn a living.

Between 1971 and 1990, while the NEP was being implemented, the economy grew at record rates. Generally speaking, economic restructuring tends to affect the economy adversely. Growth is stunted and in some communist and socialist countries the economies actually regressed. But in Malaysia the growth rate during the NEP years was consistently high, except for a short period in the middle 1980s. In view of an average growth rate of almost 7% over the twenty years of the NEP, one can only conclude that such a figure is quite a remarkable achievement for a developing country, with serious economic imbalances and even animosities between its multiracial people.

By any measure, the NEP has been a resounding success. Malaysia is today a remarkably harmonious multiracial nation, with a level of economic prosperity that is the envy of developing and even developed countries. Politically, Malaysia is stable, even though democracy provides many opportunities for destabilisation by locals and foreigners alike. If the results of the five general elections held during the NEP period are anything to go by, the Barisan Nasional Government, which implemented the NEP, has always had the support of the majority of the people from all the different communities.

The restructuring is not over. After the NEP ended in December 1990, the Government launched the ten-year National Development Policy (NDP), which stresses quality rather than quantity in the restructuring of the economic wealth of the nation. By 1997 the NDP was showing equally encouraging results. The hope is that, by the end of the NDP period at the turn of the century, the disparities between the races will have been largely eliminated.

2

The Political Dimension

A riot is at bottom the language of the unheard.
Revd Martin Luther King (1929–68)

WHEN MALAYSIA ACHIEVED independence in 1957, many predicted that the country would never be stable. Certainly, almost everyone believed that it would not prosper economically. The political marriage of convenience between the United Malays National Organisation (UMNO), the Malayan Chinese Association (MCA) and the Malayan Indian Congress (MIC), the Malay, Chinese and Indian political parties respectively, was seen as opportunistic and fragile. It would not last. It was bound to break up and the races would be at each other's throats.

In the years following the return of the British colonial administration to Malaya, in the wake of the Japanese defeat in the Second World War, relations between the Malays and the Chinese were anything but cordial. The British proposal for the Malayan Union, giving citizenship to all those resident in the Malay states and the Straits Settlements, had been violently rejected by the Malays. They did not believe that the Chinese, or the Indians for that matter, were loyal to the country, and deserved to be given the same citizenship status as themselves, the indigenous people of the Malay Peninsula. The British proposal merely heightened Malay bitterness towards the Chinese, as the Chinese communist guerrillas had attempted an armed take-over of the country in the brief interregnum between the Japanese surrender and the British reoccupation of Malaya.

The Indians had sided with the Japanese during the war, and supported the militant Indian independence fighter, Subhas Chandra Bose. The Malays did not see why the Indians, who were really more interested in India and Indian affairs, should be rewarded with citizenship of the Malayan Union. Malay concerns were not helped by the fact the Malayan Union would allow the Chinese and Indians to hold dual citizenship of Malaya and their country of origin. The final straw for the Malays was another proposal in the Malayan Union changing the status of the Malay states from British protectorates to colonies.

Malay protests led to the British abandoning the plan for the Malayan Union, instead creating the Federation of Malaya. Citizenship was granted to only a small percentage of the non-Malays. However, General Templer, the British High Commissioner, quite arbitrarily gave citizenship to 1.2 million Chinese and 150,000 Indians in 1952. Nevertheless, the Malays, who were all recognised as citizens with voting rights, continued to outnumber the eligible non-Malay voters by a high margin.

One would have thought that the Malays would have made use of their superior political position, especially as their stake in the economy was practically zero. Almost all business was in the hands of the British, other foreigners and the non-Malays, principally the Chinese. But, in spite of their recent mutual distrust and antagonism towards each other, the Malays, as represented politically by UMNO, decided to form the Alliance, first with the MCA, and then with the MIC. In the Kuala Lumpur municipal elections, held in 1952, the Alliance of UMNO and the MCA won a resounding victory. UMNO Malays supported MCA Chinese candidates in Chinese-dominated constituencies against other Chinese candidates, while in Malay-dominated constituencies UMNO candidates edged out Malay candidates from other parties with the help of Chinese MCA supporters.

In the 1955 general election, although Malay voters and Malay-dominated constituencies far outnumbered those of the non-Malays, UMNO agreed that some marginal Malay constituencies should be given to the MCA and MIC. Malay support ensured that Chinese and Indian Alliance candidates won, even if the majority of the Chinese and Indian voters preferred other candidates.

There was a very good political reason for UMNO making this sacrifice. The British had openly hinted that Malaya would not be given independence if the Malays used their political dominance to treat the Chinese and the Indians unfairly. The Malays were determined to gain independence and were prepared to make major concessions. In addition to working with the MCA and MIC, UMNO also agreed to relax the qualifications for citizenship, so that more Chinese and Indians could apply to become citizens of an independent Malaya.

The largely Malay electorate could still have rejected the Alliance candidates, particularly those who were not Malays. They could have supported the Pan Malayan Islamic Party (PMIP), or the Party Negara formed by the ex-UMNO leader, Dato Onn Jaafar. But in the 1955 election the Malays supported the Alliance so strongly that all the non-Malay candidates contesting in constituencies with Malay majorities won. Of the 52 seats contested by the Alliance in the election, only one was lost by UMNO to PMIP.

It seemed that the Malays had overcome much of their antagonism towards the Chinese, and were now willing to work with them in the political arena. The Alliance Government set to work to amend the constitution in order to give citizenship to an additional one million or so Chinese and Indians. Considering that the population of the Federation of Malaya at that time was only slightly more than five million, the agreement to give citizenship to such a large number of non-Malays was rather generous. It diluted Malay political power considerably.

The generosity of the Malays towards the Chinese and Indians removed the excuse of unfairness towards the other races, which the British were apparently going to use to deny independence to the Federation. At the same time, the remaining influence of the communists on the Chinese population in the country was undermined.

As was mentioned earlier, the Chinese communist guerrillas had attempted to take over the country by force during the interval between the Japanese defeat and the British return in 1945. This had resulted in clashes with the mainly Malay police and Malay villagers, in which many Malays lost their lives.

Fortunately, the communist attempt to take over the country was foiled. Although the British persuaded the communist guerrillas to lay down their arms, they did not in fact surrender all their weapons. They hid them, while their political wing set up the Malayan Communist Party (MCP), which took over the country's trade unions and set up various welfare and other societies amongst the Chinese population.

Through the trade unions and these societies, the communists harassed the British Military Administration (BMA). As the strength of the communists grew and they became more militant, the BMA decided to restrict their activities. Communist organisations were disbanded and their distinctive red and yellow signboards were taken down. Some of the communist leaders were detained, but most simply disappeared.

It was only too obvious that the communist leaders had returned to the jungle, and in 1948 they launched their 'armed struggle', with the killing of Malayan and British planters. The colonial authorities declared the 'Emergency' and resorted to military action against the guerrillas.

The war was not very successful at first. There were many sympathisers and active supporters for the communists amongst the Chinese population. Curfews had to be imposed, in order to prevent food and money from being supplied to the guerrillas, while illegal Chinese farmers living on the fringes of the jungle were moved out and relocated in fenced-off 'New Villages'.

In deciding to work with the MCA and give citizenship to the Chinese, UMNO was also trying to isolate the communists from the rest of the Chinese population. This strategy worked well because the majority of the Chinese seemed to appreciate the generous granting of citizenship. They supported the quest for independence, and the stand against communism. Thus the first elected Government in the history of the Malay states was able to win independence, and unite the Malays and Chinese against the communist insurrection, which brought eventual victory over the guerrillas. The special position of the Malays was also recognised.

However, euphoria over independence wore off after the first decade, as reality dawned upon the Malays. Apart from replacing the British in the administration, there had been little change in their status. They were still poor by comparison with the Chinese. The Malay leadership at the time concluded that all the Malays wanted was to become Government employees, and all the Chinese wanted was to do business. This might well have been true for the majority, but a significant number of Malays wanted the wealth they saw in business enterprises, while some Chinese felt they had a right to fill posts left vacant in the administration by the departure of the British.

As the Malays and the Chinese became more shrill in their demands for participation in each other's domain, tensions rose. The cooperation between UMNO and the MCA became strained. Attempts to give some Malays agencies for the distribution of cigarettes, for example, were opposed by the Chinese, who responded by implementing an effective boycott.

The Malays began to look more closely at the distribution of the national wealth, and concluded that they were condemned to remain poor so long as they had no meaningful participation in the business sector. There were no precise facts and figures at that time to show how wealth was distributed among the races in Malaysia. But everyone could see that the Malays had practically no stake at all in the economy. There was barely a single shop-house in Kuala Lumpur which belonged to a Malay. The signboards were all in Chinese characters, with practically nothing written in the national language.

Paradoxically, the Chinese schools were disappearing as the English schools attracted more and more Chinese students. This gave the Malays no satisfaction as the Malay medium schools had no Chinese students at all. The Malays believed that the Chinese and Indians should be forced to go to these schools at secondary level, but the Government was unwilling to force the use of the national language. Disenchantment with the UMNO-led Alliance Government increased amongst the younger Malays. At the same time, the Chinese community was not happy with the MCA, believing that the party was too accommodating to UMNO and the Malays.

There was a general assumption in the Government that matters relating to the economy and the world of finance were beyond the comprehension of the Malays. So, from the very beginning, the ministerial portfolios for finance and for commerce and industry were reserved for MCA members. The aspirations of the Malays in business and industry were hardly appreciated by these Chinese ministers. The Malays were therefore unable to make much headway in these areas.

As a result of the first Malay economic congress, held in 1965, Bank Bumiputera was established and the Rural Industries Development Authority (RIDA) was renamed the Majlis Amanah Rakyat (MARA), or the Council of Trust for the People. RIDA was an agency started by the British to persuade the Malays to accept the Malayan Union. The British had allocated RM 5 million to the agency, which was tasked largely with helping rural Malays. Scholarships were given to Malays to study shorthand in a number of commercial schools in Kuala Lumpur. After independence in 1957, RIDA's role was expanded and it started several training institutions. When RIDA was renamed, the RIDA college in Kuala Lumpur was converted to the Institute Technology MARA or ITM. In the late 1960s ITM was only a shadow of its present self, being a hotbed of agitation against the Government.

Signs of Malay and Chinese unhappiness with the Government and its policies were only too apparent, but the Government leaders refused to recognise them. The absence of open clashes between the Malays and the Chinese was taken to mean that racial harmony existed. The Alliance leaders were so confident that they went to full term before calling a general election in 1969. They also let the campaign period run the maximum six weeks. Racial issues were allowed to be discussed openly and were widely used during the campaign, by both the Malays and the Chinese.

The tension continued to mount throughout the six weeks of bitter campaigning. Politicians from all parties criss-crossed the country to rouse the people into a state of near frenzy. Every stratagem was used without thought for the consequences, particularly in terms of generating hatred between the three principal ethnic groups. The animosity between the Malays and the Chinese was noticeably exploited, in order to gain support for the parties representing them.

Many Malays in UMNO believed they could win without Chinese support. The number of Malay constituencies was large enough for a clear majority. Besides, the Malay opposition was largely represented by the extreme Malays of the Pan Malayan Islamic Party (PMIP), which was openly anti-Chinese. PMIP wanted a Malaysia ruled entirely by Malays, and used Islam as their rallying call, something which had no appeal at all to the Chinese. It was thought inconceivable that the Chinese, whether supporters of the MCA or the Chinese-based opposition, would vote for PMIP.

UMNO thought the Chinese would remain neutral, not bothering to vote at all. If the Chinese abstained, UMNO, with more Malay support, would win. They in fact wanted to win without Chinese support, so as not to feel obliged to the Chinese. They believed this would enable them to demand a more Malay-oriented government.

The Chinese in the MCA quite openly showed their desire not to support the Alliance candidates, whether Chinese or Malay. So their participation in the Alliance campaign was nominal. They also condemned the strong pro-Malay flavour of the UMNO campaign. Of course, the non-MCA Chinese made no attempt to hide their anti-Malay sentiments. Although they did not believe they could defeat the Alliance and set up a Chinese-based government, they felt that a reduction in the number of Alliance seats would undermine the political clout of the Malays.

For their part, they did not think UMNO would team up with its arch-rival PMIP. So there was no real danger of a wholly Malay government through an UMNO–PMIP coalition.

The politics of the 1969 election were entirely racial. Although the top leaders in the Alliance Government were still sanguine about events, there were clear signs that the Malay–Chinese political marriage was cracking and would soon shatter on the hard rock of emotional racialism.

Polling day on 10 May 1969 saw some strange happenings. In many constituencies where there were big Malay majorities and the rival candidates were from UMNO and PMIP, Chinese voters were seen going to the information booths operated by PMIP, to receive their registration numbers. Some UMNO officials thought this was just a ruse by the Chinese to hoodwink PMIP into thinking they would vote for them. UMNO therefore remained confident that the Chinese would either support their candidates or remain neutral. Certainly, they never believed PMIP would get the Chinese votes.

When the results were announced late on the evening of polling day, there was dismay amongst the UMNO leadership and members. In many Malay majority constituencies, UMNO had lost ground to PMIP. Even during the counting, it became clear that large numbers of Chinese were voting for the PMIP candidates. UMNO observers at the counting centres saw votes from polling stations with Chinese majorities all in favour of PMIP. With the Malay vote split between UMNO and PMIP, these Chinese votes determined the outcome in several seats, and the victors were PMIP. The UMNO assumption that the Chinese would never vote for PMIP was proved wrong. When all the results were in, the Alliance majority had been greatly reduced. The MCA had done particularly badly, indicating a major swing away from the Alliance amongst the whole Chinese community.

In a calculated gamble, the Chinese had opted for tactical voting in the Malay majority seats. But then the Chinese are inveterate risk takers. They knew that PMIP would never win a sufficient number of seats to form the Federal Government. So there was no real risk of PMIP, an Islamic party, ruling the country. On the other hand, a big victory for UMNO would truly strengthen the hand of the Malays in the Alliance Government.

The danger was always that UMNO would dump the Alliance, form a coalition with PMIP and the other Malay parties, and create a purely Malay government. The Chinese were banking on UMNO continuing to be totally opposed to PMIP, its great rival in Malay politics. UMNO and PMIP did eventually bury their differences, and PMIP, by then renamed Parti Islam Se-Malaysia (PAS), joined the UMNO-led Barisan Nasional coalition, an expanded Alliance, in 1973. The Chinese gamble paid off, but only just.

While there was a sufficient majority for the Alliance to form the Government at federal level, the ruling coalition failed to regain Kelantan from PMIP, and lost Penang to the newly formed Gerakan party. The Alliance was unable to form governments in Perak and Selangor, where it failed to win a clear majority of seats. The opposition People's Progressive Party (PPP) tried to form a coalition with PMIP in Perak, but this failed. Negotiations went on in Selangor to try and form a coalition between the Alliance and one of the minority opposition parties.

In the midst of all these political uncertainties, the opposition Gerakan was granted permission by the Government to hold a victory procession in Kuala Lumpur. Gerakan had only won in Penang, but the Chinese members wanted to celebrate what they considered their victory over the Malays. The procession deliberately passed near the Malay settlement of Kampung Baru, where insults were thrown at the Malays watching the procession.

In response UMNO demanded that they too be given permission to hold a procession in Kuala Lumpur to celebrate their victory. The Government was not in a position to deny permission, having already allowed the Gerakan procession. The

UMNO procession, however, ended in violence with the Malays attacking and killing a number of Chinese. Houses and cars were burned. At that time these were almost exclusively owned in the city by Chinese. So the Malays were confident that they were destroying only Chinese property. This point was later noted by the architects of the NEP, who felt that property, especially in urban areas, should not be owned by a single race.

An emergency was declared by the Yang di-Pertuan Agong, or the King, on the advice of the caretaker Government, which was in place during the election period. The elections due in the East Malaysian states of Sabah and Sarawak were postponed. Parliamentary government was suspended. Tunku Abdul Rahman, the prime minister, decided to let his deputy, Tun Abdul Razak, head a National Operations Council (NOC), which was empowered to take over the running of the country. The NOC included the heads of the armed forces and the police, as well as the presidents of the MCA and MIC. Similar operations councils were set up at state level.

For several weeks, sporadic violence occurred with more houses and motor vehicles being destroyed, largely by the Malays. Tun Dr Ismail, who came out of retirement to join the NOC and take charge of security matters, was totally impartial and took firm action against everyone, whether Malay or non-Malay, who violated the curfews or carried weapons. The Malays had at first believed that the attacks on non-Malays and their property would be tolerated by the largely Malay security forces. But Tun Dr Ismail soon made it clear that he wanted everyone to cease criminal activities. Within a short space of time, law and order was restored.

As peace was re-established, a debate arose as to the future of politics in Malaysia. Was the Alliance, which had actually won the election, albeit with a reduced majority, the right coalition to form the Government? The MCA had done badly in the 1969 elections, and had obviously lost the support of the majority of the Chinese. Should it continue to represent the Chinese in the

Alliance coalition? A fierce debate raged in the press over this question. Many Malays expressed the view that the MCA had failed the Alliance and should not be represented in the Government. Perhaps stung by these Malay criticisms, the MCA leader, Tun Tan Siew Sen, announced publicly that the party would not participate in the Alliance Government.

Some Malays still toyed with the idea of a wholly Malay government formed by a coalition between UMNO, PMIP and the Malay parties in East Malaysia. This would give the Malays an overall majority in the 144-seat Parliament. At state level, they also made up a majority in every state except Penang. They could prolong the emergency and rule through the NOC, where they wielded almost absolute power.

Clearly, the trend was towards a break-up of the Alliance of Chinese, Malay and Indian parties, and towards racial confrontation rather than cooperation. The future of Malaysia looked really bleak. There would be a monopoly of power by the Malays, and they would use it to grab everything for themselves, including, of course, the nation's economic wealth.

It is worthwhile noting that, despite the confusion and novelty of the various authorities set up and the action taken, both the military and the police maintained their professionalism and continued to take orders from the politicians. Yet the authority of the politicians was totally dependent on the military and the police. They could rule only so long as the men with the guns were prepared to take orders from them. In many other countries the generals or some officer class would have staged a *coup d'état*. If they had done this in Malaysia in 1969, few would have stood in their path. The police might have, but then again they might have wanted to share power with the military. In the event there was absolutely no attempt on the part of the military or the police to seize power, and to nudge or shove the politicians aside.

This is all the more amazing because the form of government, set up to deal with the situation, was actually military in character. Even the name was military. The National Operations Council was based on a military operations council, usually headed by a top military officer. It would have been perfectly natural for the Chief of the Armed Forces to ask to head the NOC. But neither General Tunku Osman nor General Dato' Ibrahim Ismail made any bid for the position, although they were amongst those who suggested the setting up of the NOC. They were quite happy to have a civilian politician, Tun Abdul Razak, chair the NOC, despite the major role played by the military and the police in restoring law and order, and in implementing the decisions of the NOC.

Although in Malaysia we take it for granted that there will not be a military regime, it should be remembered that not so very long ago, immediately after the Second World War, the country was under the British Military Administration, led by Major-General Hone. Lieutenant-General Briggs and his successor General Templer were appointed to preside over the war against the communist guerrillas, Templer combining this role with that of High Commissioner and head of the colonial administration. The situation in 1969 was tailor-made for a military take-over. That it did not happen is something Malaysians must always remember and be grateful for. Our soldiers have always been professionals, and have never harboured political ambitions, though a few have contested elections after leaving military service. For this reason, Malaysia is what it is today: a democracy ruled by civilians who are respected by the military, and who in turn respect the military and its professional role.

The proposal to set up a military-style NOC was made by a small group of public servants, which included the Chief of the Armed Forces, the Inspector-General of Police and a few senior Malay civil servants. The prime minister and the deputy prime minister were approached, and very quickly the consent of the King was obtained to declare an emergency and set up the NOC.

The NOC could have been an instrument for the Malays to take power for themselves. They had the full backing of the military and the police, which were composed largely of Malays, because few non-Malays and certainly few Chinese cared to join either the army or the police. To the credit of the Malay leaders, they never seriously considered excluding the non-Malays. Having formed the NOC with members drawn from the three major communities, the leaders decided to consult others, including the opposition, regarding the future of the country. Accordingly, a National Consultative Council (NCC) was formed, which included some members of the opposition and academics, alongside quite a number of the newly elected Members of Parliament. The NCC debated the proposals presented by the NOC to have a national ethos, or Rukunegara, and a New Economic Policy (NEP) to reduce economic disparities between the different races in Malaysia.

Clearly, the Malay leaders in the NOC were concerned not only with restoring law and order, but also with the long-term character of multiracial politics in Malaysia. The cooperation between the Malays and the Chinese, in particular during the struggle for independence, showed that, despite everything, there was a reservoir of goodwill between them. Both were apparently forward looking and both had always been pragmatic, willing to forget past conflicts and violence between them, if the necessity arose for them to work together for mutual benefit.

Although the Malays and the Chinese had been involved in ethnic violence in 1945, only seven years later they had formed the Alliance and were voting for each other's candidates in the Kuala Lumpur municipal elections. When they were collaborating to win independence from the British, there was an on-going insurrection by Chinese communists, bent on making the Malay Peninsula a Chinese-dominated communist state. A largely Malay security force was battling an almost exclusively Chinese guerrilla force. Many Malay soldiers and policemen died or were seriously wounded in the war. However, it must be acknowledged that Chinese too were killed by the communist guerrillas, having been condemned by them as traitors to their cause. Surrendered enemy personnel, almost entirely Chinese, also worked with the Special Branch to defeat the guerrillas, going as far as killing their former comrades.

The Malays, especially the political leaders, appeared to take all this into consideration, not believing in tarring all the Chinese with the same brush. They took the line that there were good Chinese and bad Chinese. The fact that some Chinese were anti-Malay, and had provoked the Malays into running 'amok' and killing people in the post-election period, did not prevent them from working with the Chinese again. Even the fact that the Chinese killed a number of Malays during the riots did not influence the decision to revive Malay–Chinese cooperation.

After getting the participation of the leaders of the MCA and MIC in the NOC, the Malay leaders set about identifying the causes of the race riots of 1969, in order to find out how to reactivate genuine Malay–Chinese cooperation in politics. The fact of race could not be ignored. The Chinese refused to be assimilated by the Malays in order to eliminate racial differences. But reducing economic disparities was possible and acceptable, if it could contribute towards lessening tension between the two communities.

Even in a homogeneous society, class divisions tend to create tension and antagonism. Thus the working classes in western countries have historically seen themselves as bitter foes of the rich or capitalist classes. It was for this reason that the communist and socialist ideologies were developed. To this day, the working classes in Europe have their own political parties, which are opposed to the rich 'conservative' parties. Very often the rivalry between different social classes has erupted into violence and civil war. In Russia the violent Bolshevik or Communist Revolution of 1917 led to the death of literally millions of people from the same ethnic group, because of class differences.

In Malaysia, prior to the NEP, it was obvious to everyone that the Malays were generally poor, while the Chinese were generally much better off. Ethnic differences have always led to conflict in any society. But when ethnic differences are reinforced by class differences, one race being poor and the other being rich, the tendency towards open and violent conflict is much higher. This was the situation in Malaysia before 1969, and there is no doubt that it was a major contributory factor to the clashes which followed the May 1969 elections.

Several piecemeal solutions were put forward, designed to increase *bumiputera* participation in the economy. Thus stalls were built in many parts of Kuala Lumpur, as soon as the riots stopped, to enable the Malays to go into petty trading. Hawking and other licences were issued to facilitate their entry into small business. But it was clear that the impact of this piecemeal approach to correcting the economic disparities between the Malays and the non-*bumiputeras* was negligible. Something had to be done on a far grander scale, and done quickly.

A number of senior Malay officials and activists were tasked by the NOC to study the problem, and to devise a solution for correcting the economic disparities between the *bumiputeras* and the non-*bumiputeras*. They came up with the NEP, which had two principal objectives:
• the eradication of poverty irrespective of race;
• the elimination of the identification of race with economic function.
The focus of the NEP was clearly not just economic but also political. It was designed to win the support of every race and to facilitate the revival of Malay–Chinese political cooperation in particular, and multiracial harmony in general.

In pursuance of this objective, Malay politicians close to Chinese leaders spent much time explaining to them the rationale and the probable results of the NEP, and its effects on Malays and non-Malays. The fact that poverty eradication was to be for all races was stressed. This, it was pointed out, meant that the NEP was not just for the Malays and the other *bumiputeras*, but for all the races in Malaysia. The other aspect of the NEP stressed to the non-Malays was that there would be no expropriation of what belonged to their communities. The wealth redistribution in favour of the Malays and the other *bumiputeras* would be from new wealth. The economic cake would be enlarged and the *bumiputeras* would get their share from this enlarged portion. It was also pointed out that, although the *bumiputeras* constituted 56% or so of the population, their share would be only 30%. The non-Malay portion would be 40% of the total.

The Malaysian economy in 1970 was divided into the traditional and modern sectors. In those days there was hardly any manufacturing industry. So the modern sector was composed of the large plantations and tin mining corporations, which were mainly foreign owned. The *bumiputeras* had to have a share of this modern sector, as their traditional occupations of *padi* farming and fishing yielded very little by way of wealth. In fact, they ensured permanent poverty. Without participation in the modern sector, there was no way for the Malays and the other *bumiputeras* to achieve the 30% share that was allocated to them. The enormity of the task was not fully appreciated at the time the NEP was formulated.

Having determined the policy, the objectives and the optimal targets, and having explained and won the support of almost everyone to the NEP, including the majority of the non-*bumiputeras*, all that remained was for the policy to be implemented. But, despite the objectives and targets being acceptable to all, insensitive implementation could still have caused political problems and rekindled racial animosities.

The NEP, as has been pointed out, was as much a political instrument as a social and economic engineering programme. Launched at the start of 1971, the NEP was given a lifetime of twenty years. In the meantime, Malaysian politics could not be left to take its own course. The NOC leaders were fully aware that, if the political situation was not conducive to the implementation of the NEP, the objectives would never be achieved. Politics therefore had to be managed during the twenty-year period, in such a way as to ensure the success of the NEP. Political instability during this period would have not only undermined the impetus behind the NEP, but also prevented the economy from growing. Quite simply, there would have been no new wealth to be redistributed.

So even as the NEP was being formulated under the emergency NOC Government, the political arena was not neglected. The leaders of UMNO set out to enlarge and consolidate the Alliance. The MCA and MIC continued to be members, as did the Sarawak and Sabah parties, which had joined the Alliance when the two states became a part of Malaysia in 1963. Preaching less politics and more development, UMNO persuaded Gerakan, which had won Penang, to join the Alliance. PAS, in control of Kelantan, also agreed to join, and so did the PPP, which wielded a great deal of influence in Perak and had so nearly succeeded in teaming up with PAS, or PMIP as the party was then called, to form the state government. The Sarawak United People's Party (SUPP) also joined, thus stabilising the often turbulent politics of that state.

The much enlarged Alliance was renamed the Barisan Nasional, or National Front, and the leaders of PAS, SUPP and Gerakan were offered ministerial posts in the cabinet. Only the Democratic Action Party (DAP) stayed out, but it was in no position to undermine the strength and cooperation of the parties in the new Barisan Nasional Government. This strength and cooperation was absolutely essential if the Government was to carry out the planned economic reforms through the affirmative action of the NEP.

With most of the original political detractors of 1969 absorbed into Barisan Nasional and anticipating full participation in the Government when Parliament was reconvened, politics, especially party politics, was much reduced. This enabled the period of rule by the NOC to be ended inside two years. Predictions that race riots would be a regular feature of multiracial Malaysia, and that the anniversary of 13 May would see another bout of blood-letting, proved baseless. There was no recurrence of the riots and violence of 1969. The fears and suspicion between the races quickly evaporated, and everyone was able to move about freely and safely in the cities and countryside.

What is often forgotten is that the race riots of May 1969 were successfully confined by the NOC to Kuala Lumpur. The rest of the country was peaceful. Chinese and Malays went about their work without fear of attack, even in areas where the majority were not from the same race. In the rural areas, where the Malays predominated, the few Chinese went about their work and business in complete safety. Similarly, in the urban areas, dominated by the Chinese, the Malays never felt unsafe. Clearly, open racial conflicts and riots were quite alien to the vast majority of people in Malaysia.

When Parliament was reconvened in February 1971, the Barisan Nasional cabinet, which included the new ministers from Gerakan, PAS and SUPP, took over from the NOC. The Barisan Nasional coalition had already obtained backing for the NEP from the NCC. When the NEP was presented to Parliament by the new Government, endorsement was achieved after some debate and criticism from the opposition, then represented almost entirely by DAP.

To progress from the near break-up of the multiracial Alliance to a new and bigger 'Alliance', which included a majority of the opposition parties, was a remarkable achievement on the part of the Malay leaders. Above all, credit for this must be given to the prime minister, Tun Abdul Razak, who overcame the reservations of the MCA to admit another Chinese-based party, Gerakan, which by implication undermined the pre-eminent position of the MCA in the Government. UMNO too had to be persuaded to accept another Malay party, PAS, which would inevitably lead to UMNO's position being eroded in Malay constituencies. In the event, UMNO's worst fears about admitting PAS were proved correct, and PAS was expelled from Barisan Nasional in 1977.

But compromise on the part of all the Barisan Nasional parties was necessary, if the nation was to focus on economic growth and a redistribution of wealth amongst the different races. Everyone appeared willing to downgrade party politics in the greater interests of the nation. With the formation of the Barisan Nasional Government, the stage was set for the serious implementation of the NEP.

The cooperation between the component parties of Barisan Nasional in the early years was real. There were no bitter altercations at either the cabinet or parliamentary levels. The members of the legislative assemblies of the states, including that of Kelantan where PAS had the majority, worked well as Barisan Nasional 'teams'. Even at grassroots level, UMNO and PAS were able to work together. Cooperation between the MCA and Gerakan proved less easy, but the effectiveness of Barisan Nasional as a coalition and government at both federal and state levels was not seriously affected. With most of the political parties in Malaysia joining Barisan Nasional, the number of Government Members of Parliament increased to over two-thirds. This enabled the Government to push through the necessary legislation and set up a variety of agencies to implement the NEP.

To return to an earlier point, insensitive implementation of the NEP could still have caused political problems and rekindled racial animosities. There were many methods of achieving the NEP 30% target for the *bumiputeras*, but not all would have been acceptable to the different races in Malaysia. If political sensitivities were not to be trampled on, the methods of implementing the NEP had to be scrutinised carefully, so as to gain the full support of all the communities and their respective political parties.

Communism and socialism were basically economic reforms in the interest of political objectives, primarily aimed at creating a more equitable society which was politically more acceptable and just. Both involved taking away from the 'haves' in order to give to the 'have-nots'. This naturally resulted in the 'haves' becoming very unhappy even when, as in some instances of socialist reform, the expropriation was largely compensated. The communists made no pretence of being fair. They simply massacred or forcibly dispossessed the 'haves' in order for the state to take over all their property. In both cases, political harmony and general well-being were not achieved. In the end, of course, both ideologies lost favour and were discarded. Their objective of creating a better society failed.

American affirmative action was and is a fairer approach, but far too many 'haves' have rejected the philosophy and justice of favouring a particular segment of the population, the blacks and the Hispanics, who have historically been disadvantaged. In this case, it is sheer selfishness on the part of these 'haves', hiding behind a misinterpretation of the principle of equality before the law. They simply ignore the fact that the law has always been discriminatory and made provision for unequal treatment, as, for example, in the differences in tax rates on the incomes of the rich and poor. In a country which has always discriminated against the blacks and the Hispanics, it is outrageous to consider that discrimination in their favour, in order to correct the effects of past discrimination against them, is unjust and contrary to the provisions of the Constitution. Outrageous or not, affirmative action faces a very uncertain future in the USA, leaving a society where disparities between the blacks and Hispanics on the one hand, and the whites on the other, have gone unredressed. In all the various sectors of the economy, blacks and Hispanics continue to be in an inferior position *vis-à-vis* the whites, and they are likely to remain permanently inferior. Indeed, the disparities will probably increase in the future.

The NEP guaranteed that implementation would not be through taking from the rich to give to the poor. Having rejected the 'Robin Hood' approach, how was wealth to be created in order to distribute it amongst the 'have-nots'?

If the wealth was created by the non-*bumiputeras*, who after all were in the best position to create it, then apportioning 30% of this wealth to the *bumiputeras* would still seem like expropriation. Besides, giving 30% to the *bumiputeras* and 70% to the non-*bumiputeras* would not reduce the disparities, but would simply perpetuate them. The wealth had therefore to be created jointly, not just by the *bumiputeras* and non-*bumiputeras*, but also by the Government, and in most instances the *bumiputeras* had to be apportioned very much more than 30%.

There were many trials and errors. Mere allocation of shares to individual *bumiputeras* resulted in most of them selling their allocated shares to the non-*bumiputeras*, in order to repay loans and enjoy quick profits. If this was the only method used, then far from the disparities being corrected, they would actually be increased.

The various states were directed to form State Economic Development Corporations (SEDCs), which were classified as *bumiputera*. They were able to start big business enterprises, usually through the allocation of Government capital, land and timber reserves for exploitation. They were also allocated shares meant for *bumiputeras* in new companies or expanding businesses. Other Government agencies were also given *bumiputera* status and pursued a similar strategy to the SEDCs. A large number of these agencies and corporations were set up, which in turn established subsidiaries and joint ventures. While these methods were politically acceptable, they did not really fulfil the objectives of the NEP. Nearly all these agencies and corporations were badly managed and lost considerable sums of money allocated to them by the Government. Only the share of the *bumiputeras* increased through these methods. Participation in business by the *bumiputeras* remained minimal.

Then the Government struck upon the idea of operating a unit trust, so as to distribute the shares of the large companies intended for the *bumiputeras* to the biggest possible number of *bumiputeras*, while preventing them from selling the shares to the non-*bumiputeras* for quick gains. Shares in the unit trust could not be sold to just anyone. Only the managers could buy back the units, if the unit holder wished to dispose of his shares.

This way the shares allocated to the *bumiputeras* would remain in a *bumiputera* agency, and could only be resold to other *bumiputeras*.

Permodalan Nasional Berhad (PNB), or the National Equity Corporation, set up to operate the unit trust, was a huge success. Further unit trusts were set up later. Today, more than five million *bumiputeras* have invested and hold shares in the various unit trusts operated by the PNB, actually making them the biggest in the world. State governments set up similar unit trusts, thus expanding further the ownership of shares by *bumiputeras* at all income levels.

Although the unit trusts enabled more shares to be retained in *bumiputera* hands, the shareholders had little involvement in the actual management of the companies in which they had shares. Their management skills and knowledge of business were not honed through this approach. Their involvement in business was too passive. Only a fortunate few learned the skills of managing unit trusts, and participated as directors in the management of the companies whose shares were held by the unit trusts.

Despite the limited exposure of *bumiputeras* to business and business practices, the Government corporations and agencies as well as the unit trusts spawned a number of capable *bumiputera* managers and entrepreneurs. These executive officers left the Government in order to go into business on their own. Some failed but others did quite well. Their appearance and successes did not go unnoticed by the Government.

If the NEP was to be a success economically and politically, there had to be proportionately the same number of big companies and entrepreneurs in both the *bumiputera* and non-*bumiputera* communities. All the strategies adopted by the Government had so far failed to produce this category of *bumiputera* businessman. But the appearance of these few *bumiputera* entrepreneurs provided the opportunity to create *bumiputera* big businesses and entrepreneurs on a scale to match those amongst the non-*bumiputera* community.

The Government seized upon the global trend towards privatisation to create the opportunities for these few *bumiputeras*, with proven track records, to go directly into big business. Against all expectations, this strategy worked and worked very well. Starting with privatisation projects, huge *bumiputera* conglomerates emerged which have been run successfully. Once started, they were able to progress on their own, with practically no Government assistance. Today, they have built up good reputations worldwide, and have gone abroad to invest and acquire foreign companies, which they have also managed successfully.

With the emergence of successful *bumiputera* entrepreneurs and executives in big business, practically all sectors of the economy now have *bumiputera* representation. The second objective of the NEP, the elimination of the identification of race with economic function, has been achieved. The first objective, the eradication of poverty irrespective of race, has also been achieved, as illustrated by the absence of unemployment in Malaysia. The economic cause of political instability in Malaysia's multiracial society has thus been largely removed.

Politically, Malaysia is a success story. It is not often that a multiracial society finds itself prosperous and stable, and also exhibits a degree of interracial harmony. As has been pointed out earlier, the expected break-up of the Alliance following the May 1969 race riots did not take place. Instead, the Alliance expanded into Barisan Nasional, of which a number of the pre-1969 opposition parties were members.

Barisan Nasional did lose PAS, but the reason was not racial or economic. PAS had used its membership of the Barisan Nasional Government to expand at the expense of UMNO. At the same time, PAS experienced an internal power struggle in Kelantan. The party was finally expelled from Barisan Nasional in 1977. In the following general election PAS lost Kelantan to UMNO. PAS recaptured the state only in 1990 after UMNO dissidents formed a new party called Semangat '46, or Spirit of '46, and made an alliance with PAS in the elections of that year. The formation of Semangat '46, like the exit of PAS from Barisan Nasional, was due not to racial or economic causes, but to an internal power struggle.

The implementation of the NEP went ahead, despite the political manoeuvres of various individuals and parties. True, the non-*bumiputera* opposition continually tried to stir up feelings amongst the non-*bumiputeras*, and even the *bumiputeras*, against the NEP. But everyone was enjoying the prosperity of the country, and they were not keen on politicising the NEP. The non-*bumiputeras* had not really lost anything due to the NEP. Instead, they were experiencing great prosperity because of the country's high growth rate.

PAS and Semangat '46 contended that the *bumiputeras* were being short-changed by the Government. They tried to prove that the non-*bumiputeras* benefited most from the NEP implementation. But the *bumiputeras* themselves were enjoying a good standard of living, as a result of the strong economic performance of the country. There was full employment, incomes had risen considerably and the *bumiputeras* were represented in all economic activities at all levels. They refused to believe that they had not benefited from the NEP.

However, it must be admitted that, by the end of the NEP period in December 1990, the quantitative and qualitative targets had not been fully achieved. In quantitative terms the *bumiputeras*, through individuals as well as the *bumiputera* agencies, had built up only a 20% stake in the corporate sector, while, qualitatively speaking, the involvement of the *bumiputeras* in the economy remained mostly at the lower end. In assessing the achievements of the NEP, the National Development Policy (NDP), launched after the end of the NEP period, must also be taken into account.

The NDP contains elements of the NEP and in many ways is an extension of it, but the emphasis is on quality rather than quantity. Indeed, most of the substantial and meaningful *bumiputera* participation in the economy has actually resulted from the focus on quality by the NDP. Yet, without the achievements of the NEP to build upon, the NDP would never have been as successful. The NDP has been equally well accepted politically by all the racial communities in Malaysia. There has been as destabilisation and economic growth has gone on unabated. From 1987 to 1996 the Malaysian economy grew at an average rate of 8%. Inflation has remained low. The success of the NDP has enabled the multiracial Barisan Nasional to continue receiving support from the people. In 1995 Barisan Nasional achieved its biggest election victory ever.

Today, Malaysia is politically much more stable even than countries with homogeneous populations. We are apt to take this for granted, but we must never forget that in the past racial clashes were not uncommon in Malaysia. We must not take the present racial harmony and political peace for granted. We must always be conscious of the need for balance and equity if the country wishes to remain stable and prosperous.

Sensitivity is necessary at all times and by everybody when dealing with race relations and disparities. The day may come when such disparities have been well and truly eliminated, so much so that everyone can feel confident of retaining and enhancing his share, whatever his race. When that day dawns, the fact of race will not be politically relevant any more. Then Malaysian politics may be based on class or ideology, regardless of race.

3

The New Economic Policy and Affirmative Action

There is nothing so bad or so good that you will not find Englishmen doing it; but you will never find an Englishman in the wrong. He does everything on principle. He fights you on patriotic principles; he robs you on business principles; he enslaves you on imperial principles.

George Bernard Shaw (1856–1950)

WHEN MALAYSIA LAUNCHED the New Economic Policy (NEP), with the objectives of eradicating poverty amongst all races and eliminating the identification of race with economic function, no one had heard of affirmative action, at least not in Malaysia. While the NEP was being implemented, we learned that there was a policy in the United States designed to correct the economic disparities between the blacks and Hispanics on the one hand, and the Caucasians or whites on the other – a policy which was referred to as affirmative action.

Apparently, it had been 'noticed' in the USA that the blacks and Hispanics did not do as well as the whites. Blacks and Hispanics were poor, and were mostly confined to low income employment. They had very few professional qualifications or working skills, and were discriminated against because of their colour and ethnic origins. They had limited access to education and training, and were therefore not upwardly mobile.

Yet the blacks and Hispanics are not inherently incapable of acquiring the knowledge and skills which could help them move up the social and economic ladder. It could be true that, due to their subculture, positive efforts to obtain knowledge and skills may be alien to them, but this is not an insurmountable problem. A determined effort to break through their cultural restraints, together with the provision of the right kind of opportunities and amenities, could change them and make them as capable as the whites in the USA. If this is done, they could join the rest of the population in availing themselves of the many and varied opportunities which their society affords, and in effect realise the American dream. The positive effort needed to achieve this goal involves discrimination in favour of the blacks and Hispanics, a discrimination to atone for past injustices against them, a discrimination which would in effect undo the results of these past injustices and return them to their rightful place in society.

If the community which is already ahead is given the same help, this will propel them even further ahead, and increase the gap between them and the more backward community. The disparities between them will never be overcome. Discrimination in favour of the blacks and Hispanics can never be considered as unfair discrimination against the whites. The blacks suffered generations of discrimination and unfair treatment at the hands of the whites. In the USA today, slavery has long since disappeared and, constitutionally at least, the blacks possess the same rights as the whites. But even now it is doubtful whether the blacks are fairly treated by the whites. There are far too many cases of ill-treatment of blacks by whites, including various notorious actions by the predominantly white police forces of cities such as Los Angeles. Yet, even if they are not ill-treated, the fact remains that the previous enslavement of the blacks and the bias displayed against the Hispanics have placed them in a very disadvantaged position in American society. They are denied the opportunity to improve their lot because they do not have the means to do so, primarily due to poverty, and also because of lingering discrimination against them.

The good life enjoyed by the whites in the USA today is due at least in part to the slavery and exploitation of the blacks in the past. What the whites have now, including the advantages they still hold over the blacks and Hispanics, amounts to the inheritance of ill-gotten gains from their forefathers, irrespective of whether their own forefathers had slaves or ill-treated the Hispanics, or not. The slaves in the south and later the cheap black labour force of the north laid the foundations for the present prosperity of the USA, maybe not entirely but certainly to some extent. Part of what the whites of America enjoy today derives from the sweat and tears of the black slaves and the freed blacks after the abolition of slavery in 1863. It must always be remembered that, long after slavery was abolished, the blacks continued to be exploited.

Discrimination in favour of the blacks should therefore be regarded as a form of over-correction, which would be likely to place them in a position as favourable as that of the whites. At that stage, positive discrimination may no longer be necessary. This is what affirmative action in the USA is all about. It is an attempt to counter the results of negative action, in the form of the enslavement and decades of prejudice against the blacks and, more recently, prejudice against the Hispanics too. Sometimes, the end result does justify the means, and to reject the means and so perpetuate an injustice would seem to be carrying out a principle without political or common sense.

The spurious argument that positive discrimination on the basis of race or colour is contrary to the American Constitution is untenable. In the first place, the Constitution is not God's law. It was merely a very human attempt to bring about a kind of justice in an unjust situation. Man's perception of justice has never been perfect because, at any point in time, the prevailing situation is regarded as the epitome of justice. Thus, when slavery was permitted, society actually and honestly believed it was right and proper. Some people were deemed superior to other people, and had the right to lord it over them. In ancient Greek democracy only a select group of people were considered entitled to participate in government. Slaves, women and those citizens without land were left outside the political process. This was considered absolutely right and absolutely just.

Women in Britain only won the right to vote after the First World War. Before the efforts of the suffragettes and the sterling work of women during the war, British politicians of all shades of opinion felt women had no claim to such a right. Universal suffrage is a very recent phenomenon, so recent that the Swiss only gave women the right to vote some two decades ago. The evolution of citizens' rights is still going on.

While the denial of rights has been regarded as just in the past, so the granting of excessive rights to a particular class or group has also been considered just and fair. When only landowners participated in government, it was undoubtedly a case of a particular group in society possessing excessive rights. The political system came into disrepute, and a reaction set in, with other groups seeking change through either revolution or constitutional reform. But the pendulum has, in certain instances, swung too far, depriving the privileged of their rights by giving excessive rights to the underprivileged.

At one time, workers, both agricultural and industrial, were without rights. They were thoroughly exploited by their feudal and, later, their capitalist 'lords'. The workers fought a long and valiant struggle for fairer treatment. They finally succeeded through unionising, and devising a variety of effective industrial actions. As the trade unions grew in strength and amalgamated, the power of the workers increased dramatically. From being an underprivileged group in society, the workers, through combining, had developed into a highly influential group, more powerful than their employers. The concept of justice was revised, and soon the privileges of the workers became rights, considered just and absolutely proper by the rest of society, and usually enshrined in legislation.

The basic aim of any trade union has always been to improve working conditions for its membership through collective bargaining with the employer. But from the start there were intellectuals and union leaders who viewed the labour movement as a means to effect fundamental changes in society. These communists and socialists seized power either through force of arms or the ballot box, and then in turn discriminated against their former employers. The communists massacred those who had lorded over them, while the socialists nationalised the industries and landholdings of the former privileged groups. All this was done in the name of justice. Today, we see such actions as an injustice. But for the communists and socialists what they did was in the interests of social and economic justice. To discriminate in favour of the workers was for them right and proper.

This digression is intended to illustrate that concepts of fairness and justice are neither perfect nor permanent. What is fair and just in one period of history may be considered grossly unfair and an injustice in another period, while what is considered fair and just in one society or country can certainly be considered unfair and unjust in another society or country. No one, at any time or in any place, has a right to claim that only his values are absolutely valid and proper. He may, indeed, change his mind later. A judgement made questioning the constitutionality of affirmative action in the USA may sound fair and just from the point of view of the whites, but in fact it can be argued and demonstrated that such an attitude is unfair and unjust. In Malaysia the NEP, which involves affirmative action in favour of the *bumiputeras*, is not considered unjust by the majority of the people. Such an approach may be regarded as an injustice in the eyes of those in the West, who subscribe to the concept of justice as developed there. But the NEP is a policy designed to correct an injustice resulting from past policies and actions in Malaysia.

To understand the basis of the NEP, one has to look back into the history of Malaysia, to the period when Malaya, as the country was then known, was a de facto colony of the British. This period coincided with the practice of slavery in the USA, when thousands upon thousands of Africans were captured, shipped to the North American mainland in appalling conditions, and sold there like animals into a life of slavery.

In Malaya the British made no attempt to work with the Malays and the other *bumiputeras*, or indigenous people. The British certainly did not make any special effort to educate or train them. Thus they were unable to participate in the new colonial administration or commercial life, as practised by the British East India Company and the later British merchant houses. The *bumiputeras* naturally did not extend full cooperation to their colonial masters, preferring to continue with their own way of life, as befitted the 'sons of the soil', the definitive people of the Malay states.

In North America, the British brought in slaves from Africa to provide labour on the plantations and farms, while in the Malay states they imported indentured Indian labourers to work on the rubber estates. Later, when the need arose for clerical and other low-grade staff in the government and the British plantation, mining and trading companies, more Indians and Ceylon Tamils were shipped in to meet the demand. Since the British did not intend settling in the Malay states, as they did in Australia, New Zealand and Southern Africa, deterred probably by the tropical climate, they encouraged Chinese immigration to work the tin mines and establish supporting commercial infrastructures, such as the retail business network.

In the five Unfederated Malay States the sultans were able to prevail on the British to employ Malays in government service, a practice which amply demonstrated that Malays could be trained at least for administrative and clerical work. But in the Federated Malay States and the Straits Settlements, there were hardly any Malays in the colonial government service, except as 'orderlies', working as office boys and drivers.[1]

Although there were a number of government schools for non-Europeans, there were far more non-Malay than Malay students. The Chinese and Indians gave greater priority to education than the Malays, many of whom were reluctant to lose the services of their children in the fields and home. Most Malay boys received only a primary education, whereas most Malay girls did not go to school at all. The standards in the government Malay schools were never more than rudimentary, the teachers being poorly qualified and largely untrained. The Malays were also suspicious of any schools run by foreigners and which did not teach the Koran. The schools set up by the various Christian missions actively discriminated against the Muslim Malays, particularly

---

[1] The Federated Malay States – Selangor, Perak, Negeri Sembilan and Pahang – were brought together as a federation of British protectorates in 1896, with effective power residing in the hands of a British resident-general. The Unfederated Malay States – Johor, Kedah, Perlis, Terengganu and Kelantan – remained outside this colonial federation, although by 1914 they had all fallen under direct British influence.

where scholarships were involved. To be fair, they also discriminated against non-Christian non-Malays. Scripture was one of the compulsory subjects for all students attending the mission schools.

As part of British colonial policy, the sons of Malay aristocrats and members of the Malay royal houses were sent to England to study. Few obtained any worthwhile university qualification, but many in the process lost their Malay cultural roots. As far as possible, they tried to adopt British and European ways.

In Sarawak and British North Borneo, now Sabah, the Christian missions operated schools where active proselytising was carried out. Although this enabled non-Malay, non-Muslim *bumiputeras* to obtain a very basic education, little attempt was made to provide secondary or university education to any of the indigenous population. Consequently, at the time of independence, the educational achievements of the *bumiputeras* were even lower in Sarawak and Sabah than in the Malay Peninsula, with practically nobody having a university education.

Although it was more subtle, British policy in Malaya, Sarawak and Sabah was no less discriminating against the *bumiputeras* than the white European settlers were against the Red Indians in North America. The tendency to introduce non-indigenous people to help the process of colonisation was partly determined by the knowledge that it was easier to manage non-indigenous people in an alien land than the local population. The non-indigenous immigrants were initially disoriented, and always felt threatened by the possibility of being repatriated or becoming unemployed in a strange land. At home, they had not been gainfully employed or had earned only a meagre living, so they were usually better off in their new country. They might still want to go home, but only after they had accumulated a decent nest egg. All of these factors made them docile and willing to work, indeed work hard, to ensure that their colonial employers retained their services.

We see a similar phenomenon amongst foreign workers in

Malaysia today. They are more easily managed and more productive than many of the locals. They seldom complain about their treatment or the lower wages they are paid. For these reasons, employers generally prefer foreign to indigenous workers.

In Malaysia, as in other British colonies in Africa and the South Pacific, the wide usage of migrant or indentured labour retarded the development of the indigenous people. As was stated earlier, this was a form of discrimination against the *bumiputeras*. It is therefore only right to discriminate now in their favour, so as to undo the adverse effects of previous discrimination during British colonial rule.

Some maintain that the present generation should not be made to atone or to compensate for any injustices perpetrated by their forefathers. They argue that the past is past and, if the descendants of the people who suffered in the past are still suffering as a result of past treatment, that is no reason for taking special action which might discriminate against others. It is sufficient that the discriminatory practices of the past have been discontinued, and everyone is now treated as equals.

But the damage resulting from past discrimination against a people is much more than the practice of non-discrimination can repair. Even if equal treatment is meted out, disadvantaged people cannot derive the same benefits as those who have never been disadvantaged, and people who have been discriminated against for centuries cannot be anything but disadvantaged. In one of the popular clichés of modern times, creating a 'level playing field' is not sufficient to ensure fair competition, when the contestants are not equally matched. Only when the contestants are in the same league or class will a 'level playing field' result in fair competition and fair results.

Years of discrimination do not only affect the development of knowledge, experience and skills. Allied to decades and centuries in which a people have been incapable of competing and succeeding, discrimination also affects the minds of the people concerned. They become dispirited and lose all self-confidence. They develop a deep inferiority complex, with an inner feeling that they are just incapable of doing what others can do. They have no capacity to compete and may even lose the will to try.

The Malays and the other *bumiputeras* of Malaysia developed a deep conviction that there were certain things they just could not do, even if they were given a chance and even if they really tried. Most Malays were convinced that they were inherently incapable of doing business, and could not be methodical, or understand scientific and mechanical matters. Such was their conviction about their lack of these skills that, except for the European colonisers, they ascribed these skills exclusively to the Chinese and Indians. They always talked of Chinese or Indian shops (*kedai China, kedai Keling*), Chinese craftsmen (*tukang China*) and so on. In a well-known Malay nursery rhyme, the child is made to accept as a matter of fact that shops belong to the Chinese:

> *Buai laju-laju*
> *Sampai balik sana*
> *Beli baju baru*
> *Dari kedai China*
> (Swing and swing fast
> Till the other side
> Buy a new dress
> From a Chinese shop)

A shop is not just a shop, it has to be a Chinese shop. The truth was that, after decades of British rule, Malay shops had disappeared even in Malay villages. Apart from the occasional Indian one, all shops were Chinese.

The colonisation of a country and its indigenous people is not just a matter of physical occupation, and overlordship in matters of administration, legislation and taxation. It is also a colonisation of the minds and the psychological make-up of the people colonised. When such a colonisation is accompanied by active discrimination against the subject people, with their exclusion from the development of knowledge and skills, and from the mainstream of life, the damage inflicted is much more severe. When this type of colonisation persists for decades and centuries, the culture and whole psyche of the people become terribly weakened.

The Malays from the great 15th-century kingdom of Melaka had initially poked fun at the *Bengali Puteh* (White Bengalis), their name for the Portuguese, who were the first Europeans they came into contact with. These Malays were the citizens of a vigorous, independent state, used to dealing with foreigners from as far away as India, China and the Middle East. At that time, Melaka was the greatest emporium in the East and centre of the valuable spice trade. The Malays collected port taxes and administered the laws of the country, but, above all, they excelled at trade. They had their complex etiquette and traditions, their own political system and great wealth. In Melaka and the surrounding lands, the Malays were the lords and masters, equal and even superior to all foreigners and certainly not inferior to anyone.

Over four hundred years of European colonisation followed, destroying Malay confidence and self-respect. Colonised physically and mentally, they accepted anything and everything that was imposed upon them by the colonial powers. After the Portuguese, they submitted to the Dutch, the British and even the Japanese, with only sporadic and limited resistance. They could not think of themselves as being independent any more.

The Malays came to feel inferior to everyone, including the Indians and Chinese brought to Malaya by the British. True, they did maintain a sense of proprietorship over the country, though only just. Had it not been for their outrage at the prospect of losing this through the Malayan Union proposal, they might never have asserted themselves and eventually pushed for independence. They were, in fact, ready to welcome back the British after the defeat of Japan, and return to the situation which prevailed before the Pacific War and the Japanese Occupation of the Malay Peninsula.

At the time of the struggle for independence, the Malays were divided. Some among the social élite in the Malay states continued to believe they could never be independent. They had become too dependent upon the British, the colonial masters, and the economic role and services of the Chinese and Indians.

Even after independence was achieved, many of the Malay leaders clung to the colonial apron-strings, allowing the country to follow slavishly the foreign policies and defence strategies of the former colonial masters. They believed the most they could claim for themselves was the role of passive administrators, filling the posts left vacant by the departure of the British colonial officials. The economy, business, trade and the professions were not for them. The Chinese and Indians would continue to dominate in these areas.

But a few Malays were not so easily satisfied with what amounted to a mere change of administrative personnel. They wanted to reclaim their lost dignity and their identity as a people. Some, of course, yearned to restore the full glory of Melaka and the other Malay empires of the past; to undo everything that the colonial powers had done, and become once more the definitive people of the Malay land, *Tanah Melayu*. Others felt a need to accept the reality of a multiracial Malaysia. The country had changed. What regained independence was not old Melaka or Kedah or Johor-Riau, or any of the Malay empires. This was a totally new entity, a federation of Malay states whose people were multiracial, whose politics were no longer feudal but democratic, and whose major problem was the disparities in social and economic terms between the races. These disparities were given greater emphasis by the physical division into rural and urban, as well as the differences in religion, culture and language.

Any analysis after the fact must be empirical, but such analysis is no less valid simply because it is empirical. The Malays who rioted in May 1969 did not analyse their own psyche and the

79

historical causes of their actions. They simply reacted to their fears and frustrations, their feelings of betrayal at the hands of the people they had accepted as partners, to whom they had conceded many things, but whom they now felt had failed them.

It would have been only too easy for the Malay leaders in the aftermath of the 1969 riots to pander to these extreme views, take power and seek a return to total and absolute Malay domination. But they did not. They chose instead to redress the Malay grievances, without going back on the undertaking given to the non-Malay citizens of the country in the Constitution.

Tun Abdul Razak and the other Malay leaders decided simply to restructure the economy, so that the *bumiputeras* would have their share of the nation's wealth. They believed that it was the economic disparities which lay at the root of the trouble, and that, if these disparities were corrected, the Malays and the other *bumiputeras* would be able to live together with the non-*bumiputeras* in peace. They were not too ambitious, for they wanted the *bumiputeras*, who constituted 56% of the population, to control only 30% of the nation's economic wealth, as represented by the business sector of the country. They agreed that the Chinese and the Indians should have more with 40%, while foreigners, predominantly the former colonial masters who had gained from having privileged access to land and wealth, and were not citizens at all, should only have their share reduced from 60% to 30%. The Malay leaders also agreed there should be no discrimination between race when it came to poverty eradication. In a land flowing with milk and honey, no one of whatever race should be poor.

So the NEP was formulated with the twin objectives:
• the eradication of poverty irrespective of race;
• the elimination of the identification of race with economic function.

In actual fact, the NEP was only a moderate form of affirmative action. The end result would still not be completely fair to the disadvantaged *bumiputeras*. Only diehard racists and believers in the 'winner takes all' principle or 'everyone for himself' could consider the NEP as unfair and unjust. The NEP was roughly the embodiment of the affirmative action approach formulated in the USA, which has had such mixed fortunes in recent years.

The Government planners and policy-makers did not realise the enormity of the task they had set out to accomplish. In the first place, they had given a solemn undertaking that the redistribution of wealth would not be achieved through expropriation of what belonged to the other races, so as to allow the redirection of resources to the poorer sections of the population. Expropriation was, of course, the way adopted by the communists and the socialists. Yet socialism, if not communism, was for a long time regarded as a very respectable political creed, even by the pontificating West. Surely, the concept and achievements of the NEP should be accorded more respect in the West and the world at large.

If wealth was to be made accessible to the less privileged, it still had to come from somewhere. The Government planners decided that it should be new wealth. The economic cake had to be made larger, and out of the new portion the *bumiputeras* would be given a bigger share, so that their economic growth would be faster. It had to be faster if the *bumiputeras* were going to catch up with the non-*bumiputeras*. If the two groups had grown at the same rate, the disparities would have not only remained, but actually increased.

In 1970 the *bumiputeras* controlled only 2.4% of the nation's economic wealth, with 1.6% of that being held by individuals and the rest by trust agencies. The non-*bumiputeras* had 34.3%. If both *bumiputera* and non-*bumiputera* wealth grew by 100%, the economic gap between the two communities would continue to widen. Even if *bumiputera* wealth grew by 100%, while non-*bumiputera* wealth grew by only 10%, the gap would still widen. At the same time, the whole economy would be growing. A growing economy was, of course, essential for the success of the NEP, but this would also make it more difficult to raise the *bumiputera* share. Moreover, the NEP had only twenty years to achieve more than a twelvefold increase in the *bumiputera* share of the nation's wealth, in the context of an economy which, if it grew at an average of 7% per annum, would double in capacity every ten years.

Allocating a certain percentage of the nation's economic wealth to the *bumiputeras* was clearly far easier than achieving the target figure set. It was not simply that the target might be too ambitious. The expectation that a people, who were not qualified or experienced in business, could actually achieve a higher rate of growth than those who were already very highly qualified was in reality rather unrealistic.

As was pointed out earlier, the *bumiputeras* not only lacked the essential skills in business, but also suffered from a debilitating lack of self-confidence. Even if they were given the opportunities and the support, even if there was positive discrimination in their favour, it was never certain that they could avail themselves of the opportunities and succeed.

At the same time, the Government planners themselves were not quite sure how to implement the NEP objectives. They distributed contracts, licences, import permits, shares and so on to the *bumiputeras* indiscriminately. They set up Government business corporations, and then directed business to these corporations. They created monopolies. They set up agencies and statutory bodies, which were run by civil servants who really did not understand how to manage business. However, some positive results were achieved in terms of the *bumiputeras* having a greater share of the economic cake. Whereas very few shares in public or private limited companies had been owned by the *bumiputeras*, the implementation of the NEP led to shares in various companies being allocated to and purchased by the *bumiputeras* or those institutions set up by Government to represent their interests.

As the years passed and the NEP gained momentum, more innovative methods of economic redistribution were devised and adopted. All of them involved some degree of discrimination in favour of the Malays and the other *bumiputeras*. With each innovation, further progress was made towards the objectives. Better still, the implementation of the NEP and the accompanying discrimination did not affect economic growth. In fact, Malaysia's economic growth actually accelerated. Between 1971 and 1990, despite a recession in the mid-1980s, the average growth rate was almost 7%, well in excess of the country's population growth.

Malaysians were living a more affluent lifestyle, with generally higher incomes for everyone. Unemployment was reduced to zero, and poverty was almost entirely eradicated. No one felt deprived because of the NEP, even though there was discrimination. This was because there was more than enough for everyone. Indeed, there was enough even for foreigners, so that in a country with only 20 million people, foreign workers totalled 2 million. Neither were they all low-income labourers. Many foreign professionals and executives found jobs in Malaysia, being employed not only by foreign companies, but also by local businesses.

The NEP may not have been the direct cause of the increase in wealth, but it certainly did not stifle the economic growth of the nation, and therefore the creation of more wealth. Affirmative action, it seems, can not just result in a redistribution of wealth favouring the disadvantaged, but can also go hand in hand with growth in prosperity for the whole nation, including those not receiving special treatment.

No one in Malaysia thought of challenging the NEP in the courts for discrimination. Some tried to work up political feelings against the NEP, but the continued strong support for the governing Barisan Nasional coalition, which formulated and implemented the NEP, indicated that the NEP was an affirmative action which Malaysians of all races supported to the full.

It was pointed out earlier that popular perceptions of justice can differ greatly. The reverence attributed to the law by some legislators and legal experts has led them to close their eyes when the law results in an obvious injustice. Instead of negating or revising laws which result in injustices, they take their stand on the sanctity of the law. Everybody needs the rule of law, but that must not blind us to the fact that laws can result in injustice.

If one looks at some of the laws of the Middle Ages, one cannot consider that they were just. People were being hanged for even minor crimes, including stealing sheep, while, as recently as the 19th century, western European countries were handing down the death penalty for innumerable offences. The death penalty is still carried out today in many states of the USA, though most western countries have abolished it, believing capital punishment to be inhuman.

Clearly, perceptions of what constitutes justice have changed and changed again and again over the centuries. The people who today condemn affirmative action as being an unjust form of discrimination are practically the same as those people who in the past upheld the cruel practice of slavery and, after abolition, perpetuated segregation and persecution through such things as the notorious Jim Crow laws. Their new perception of justice is based entirely on equal treatment for all, irrespective of the end results. The means are important; the end result is of no consequence to them.

Interestingly, it is these same people who talk incessantly of a 'level playing field' as the epitome of fair play. It does not matter if the contestants are unevenly matched, if the contest is between giants and midgets, if the giants are experts and the midgets are beginners. So long as the playing field is level, the result must be considered fair. If the midgets are expected to lose, and do in fact lose, the result is still considered fair because the playing field is level. Yet those who adhere to the fairness of the level playing field happily accept handicaps when they play golf! They do not think there is any contradiction in their thinking.

In Malaysia we accept that the disadvantaged must be given some special consideration. Not only must the playing field be level, but the players must be evenly matched. If they are not evenly matched, handicaps will be given – a form of discrimination in favour of the disadvantaged and against the advantaged or scratch players. Justice in Malaysia must also take into consideration any mitigating circumstances. What is important is not blind adherence to a principle, but that the principle itself makes allowance for the possibility that its application may result in the very thing it is trying to prevent.

Malaysia's NEP was a form of affirmative action, a form which stressed the results. Here was an instance where the end justified the means. Having admitted that the distribution of wealth between the different races in the country was unfair, we were willing to be unfair, in order to achieve fair results and the equitable distribution of wealth.

4

Growth with Equity

A house divided against itself cannot stand.

Abraham Lincoln (1809–65)

THE NEW ECONOMIC Policy (NEP) was never about equal wealth for every Malaysian citizen, but rather the creation of proportionate wealth distribution between the different racial communities in the country. What the non-*bumiputeras* had, the *bumiputeras* also had to have. This meant not only proportionate wealth, but also proportionate poverty.

Of course, it would have been easier to equalise the wealth of all the communities by ensuring that every Malaysian possessed the same amount of wealth. This would certainly have given the *bumiputeras* and the non-*bumiputeras* a proportionate equal share of the nation's wealth. However, the various attempts in the past by communists and socialists to redistribute wealth equally amongst all the people resulted only in equal poverty and not equal wealth. In the process, the countries concerned also became poor. The NEP was never intended to redistribute wealth equally to the different racial communities, at the expense of national economic expansion and prosperity. The objective was to achieve growth with equity, or, in other words, to create more wealth and distribute it, in order to correct the imbalances between the different communities and not between individual citizens.

Growth was a prerequisite for the success of the NEP. The resources needed to correct the imbalances between the racial communities had to come from the creation of new wealth, generated by the expansion of existing businesses or the start of new ones. If this correction was to be achieved, it was necessary to allocate more of the new wealth to the *bumiputeras* than to the non-*bumiputeras*, who already controlled a much larger proportion of the country's economic cake. To give equally to both groups or, worse still, to give in accordance with the capability to acquire wealth would certainly have increased rather than reduced the disparities.

This corrective redistribution of wealth was not easily achieved. If a non-*bumiputera* business expanded or a new company was started, giving more of the shares created to the *bumiputeras* might result in them holding the majority of the stock. This would not be acceptable to the non-*bumiputeras*. They would be losing control of their own businesses, which in a way amounted to expropriation. On the other hand, if a bigger share allocation was given to the non-*bumiputeras*, who of course already had a larger stake, this would not correct the imbalances between the racial communities at all. Indeed, they would increase.

The situation with foreign-owned companies was even worse. They did not want to have any *bumiputera* participation when they initiated new investments or expanded their existing businesses. Without *bumiputera* involvement, their share of the national wealth, estimated at 60% in 1970, was likely to get even larger.

In 1970 the *bumiputeras* possessed only 2.4% of the country's wealth, while the non-*bumiputeras* had 34.3%. Bringing the *bumiputera* share up to 30%, the principal target of the NEP, involved an increase of 1250%. Meanwhile, increasing the non-*bumiputera* share to 40%, the figure stipulated under the NEP, meant an increase of only 16%. Obviously, far less effort was required to achieve the NEP target for the non-*bumiputeras* than for the *bumiputeras*. If this 1250% increase for the *bumiputeras* was to come from economic growth alone, the target seemed quite unattainable, especially if they were allocated only 30% from each new business or expansion of business. While a growing economy was essential for the success of the NEP, this made the task even more difficult. During the years of the NEP, the Malaysian economy actually achieved a GDP growth rate of almost 7% per annum. Not only had the *bumiputera* share of the national wealth to grow from 2.4% to 30% over this period, but the 30% in 1990 had to be much bigger in absolute terms than the 30% in 1971.

The NEP antedated the switch of the command economies of the communist eastern bloc to the free market system at the end of the 1980s. After at least forty years of communist control, the people in these countries had no business skills or managerial experience. They had no capital and technology or expertise of their own. Perhaps most damaging of all, personal or local initiative had been anathema to the communist regimes, and had been totally repressed.

The communist countries had, of course, restructured in the past by expropriating the wealth and businesses of the owners of the 'means of production'. These people were no longer alive. There was little or no private capital and there were no managers familiar with the free market. The state-owned banks were conditioned to operating in a command economy and could not be easily privatised. Commercial banking was simply unknown. How were these countries suddenly going to enter business in a big way and replace the old state enterprises?

The governments tried many approaches, but most of them failed. The closure of backward state-owned enterprises resulted in massive unemployment. Meanwhile, the cost of living rose rapidly, as the governments removed subsidies on essential items such as food, housing, transport and clothing, and allowed the free market to determine prices. The asset value of the potentially profitable state companies, earmarked for privatisation, naturally increased. But, in most instances, private citizens had no money to buy a stake in these enterprises.

The result of the attempt to switch from a command to a market economy in most of the former communist countries was not prosperity but economic regression. Unemployment went on rising, while rampant inflation undermined pensions and the wages of those who still had jobs. There was in fact a yearning amongst many people to go back to the communist command system and the subsidies it was based on. In a few countries, notably the Czech Republic, Hungary and Poland, the switch to a free market system did succeed. But these were the more fortunate countries – fortunate in terms of their national resources, their proximity to Germany and the centre of European economic power, and the productivity of their workforces. The governments raised money for investment through the issue of bonds, while the state-owned businesses were sold off at nominal prices. Only a few citizens were able to buy controlling interests in and manage the major enterprises, but the majority could still purchase shares in these companies or set up small businesses of their own.

There were obvious similarities between the situation in the communist countries, at the time of their switch to a free market economy, and that prevailing in the *bumiputera* community in Malaysia when the NEP was launched. There were no *bumiputera* entrepreneurs or managers possessing the kind of skills required to make restructuring a success, and there was no *bumiputera* capital. But there was also one significant difference. Whereas the position was the same for everybody in the communist countries, the *bumiputeras* had to face competition from those already familiar with the workings of the capitalist system, and who were rich in capital and economically sophisticated. Without some help the *bumiputeras*, largely peasants and fishermen, were bound to fail.

Hence there was a need for affirmative action to bring the *bumiputeras* into the mainstream of Malaysian economic life. The *bumiputeras* had to be favoured in terms of access to capital, licences, permits, contracts and the distribution of shares. Without this favourable treatment, the NEP would have failed.

Again it must be emphasised that the NEP was not intended to distribute wealth equally amongst the *bumiputeras*, but to achieve equality in the distribution of wealth between the *bumiputeras* and the non-*bumiputeras*. Just as there were wealthy and poor non-*bumiputeras*, so there also had to be a proportionate number of wealthy and poor *bumiputeras*. In addition, there had to be no division between *bumiputeras* and non-*bumiputeras* in terms of employment. *Bumiputeras* had to be represented in the same proportions as non-*bumiputeras*, if possible, in every job and profession at all levels.

If this redistribution was not to be carried out from expropriated wealth, the first essential requirement was growth. This meant that the business climate had to be suitable for economic activity by everybody, *bumiputeras*, non-*bumiputeras* and foreigners alike. Priority was initially given to the creation of jobs in areas where the *bumiputeras* were poorly represented: for example, in manufacturing. This was simply done by providing incentives for foreign investment in the labour-intensive manufacturing sector. Employment was created for both non-*bumiputeras* and *bumiputeras*, although the latter tended to make up the majority because the new jobs were largely low paid and required simple skills.

In time these labour-intensive industries absorbed all the available workers from all the communities. This helped achieve the first NEP objective: the eradication of poverty amongst all races in Malaysia. At the same time, it also helped to remove the identification of race with economic function, at least in the manufacturing sector.

However, if the 30% target for the *bumiputera* share of the national wealth was to be achieved, there had to be a much higher growth rate in the *bumiputera* part of the economy than in that belonging to the non-*bumiputeras*. This was never going to be easy. New or expanded non-*bumiputera*-owned enterprises had naturally to involve a larger share for the non-*bumiputeras* than the *bumiputeras*. Since the non-*bumiputeras* already had a bigger part of the economic cake, even giving the *bumiputeras* 30% would not bring the overall *bumiputera* share up to 30%. The answer was obvious: the *bumiputera* share in non-*bumiputera* companies would have to exceed 30%, while remaining less than the non-*bumiputera* share. At the same time, there had to be more *bumiputera*-owned or majority-owned companies, particularly large-scale ventures in terms of capital, if the NEP was going to make a significant difference to the distribution of shareholdings in Malaysia.

The opportunity came when the Government decided to privatise state-owned companies and services. After a decade or more of the NEP, a number of *bumiputera* managers and entrepreneurs had emerged, although they still had no track record of managing really big enterprises. In Permodalan Nasional Berhad (PNB) some *bumiputeras* had been appointed as chief executive officers and managers of companies with considerable PNB shareholdings, but they were not fully in charge. They were not shareholders and were not risking their own capital.

The first major test was the privatisation of the North–South Highway. Renong, a *bumiputera* company which owned a controlling share of the New Straits Times Press and also had a shareholding in TV3, then the only privately owned Malaysian television company, made a bid for the 800 km highway running from Johor Bahru in the south of the country to Bukit Kayu Hitam, located on the border with Thailand.

The negotiations over the terms of the privatisation were complex, involving the period of the concession, the toll rates to be charged and the provision of soft loans. If the full value of the partly built North–South Highway had been demanded by the Government, there would have been no possibility for any private operator, *bumiputera* or non-*bumiputera*, to make any profit at all after servicing the loans, both soft and commercial, much less give any return to the Government for the concession.

But if the Government continued owning the North–South Highway, finished the construction of the whole project and collected the tolls, there was no prospect of recouping the capital outlay already spent, let alone the sums required for completion. The Government was also facing other maintenance and development demands on its limited resources, both for other infrastructure projects and for social services, which had first call on any available funds. The simple truth was that, if the Government depended on its own finances and loans, the Highway would never be completed or, at best, would be built very slowly. This meant that the Malaysian people would continue to be denied the use of an essential road, linking the major cities and towns of the west coast of the Malay Peninsula. The Government would not earn anything worthwhile, if it continued to own and tried to complete the Highway. By privatising it, even at a nominal price, the Government would not be losing anything. Indeed, this represented a saving on further capital expenditure and the losses incurred by the unprofitable operation of the Highway.

Although the Government had decided to privatise infrastructure, this did not mean that it could just wash its hands completely of the enterprises concerned. The taxes paid by the people had to be returned, at least in part, through the provision of essential utilities. If the Government sold off infrastructure at the full price, the rates or charges would inevitably be very high in order for the private operator to recover the huge capital outlay. This would be a burden on the taxpayers. Indeed, it was always doubtful whether, at such rates, the services would be popular enough to earn sufficient return for the new operator.

The Government had to transfer the assets of the utilities at a nominal price and even provide soft loans, in order to keep the rates low and affordable, as well as to allow the private operator to pay off its debts and earn a profit. Moreover, the private operator was expected not only to maintain the utility concerned in a good serviceable condition, but also to improve and extend it when required. The sale at below net asset value and the provision of soft loans were therefore not just to help the operator, but also for the benefit of the people in terms of lower rates and charges. This was regarded by the Government as maintaining its obligation to the Malaysian taxpayers.

The private operator was not allowed to sack employees, in order to reduce operating costs. Instead, the employees were offered better pay than they were receiving in Government service. They were also entitled to buy a significant percentage of shares at the original offer price, and to receive bonuses when the company started to make a profit.

As if these conditions were not enough, in most cases the

Government sold off only enough shares to enable the newly privatised company to be listed as a public limited company. This was done to allow the Government to take advantage of any increase in the share price when disposing of further tranches in the future. In this way, Government earnings from the sale could approach, and indeed exceed, the original market value of the enterprise, or even the net asset value.

All of these factors, together with the relatively short concession periods granted, where applicable, made the privatised projects less profitable than many believed they were. Since the privatisation policy was an important part of NEP restructuring, i.e. to give the *bumiputeras* a larger share of the companies in order to achieve the target of 30% share ownership, it was vital that the new *bumiputera* entrepreneurs ran the companies profitably. Considering that they had little experience in running such large companies on a purely commercial basis, it is gratifying to see how well they have done.

Privatisation was by far the most important means of enhancing the *bumiputera* share in the commercial life of the nation. The privatisation projects did not always go to individual *bumiputeras* or their companies. In many instances, the PNB bought up the Government-owned entity through one of its many subsidiaries, some of which were set up specifically for the purpose, either fully owned or as a joint venture. Among the first of these joint ventures was the Kelang Container Terminal. Later North Port was also transferred to the PNB.

The intention was not that PNB should retain these companies permanently. Although they were largely profitable, the capacity of PNB to manage them innovatively was limited. The *bumiputeras* put in charge of the individual companies had not invested their own money, being professional managers rather than entrepreneurs. Yet the NEP demanded as many *bumiputera* entrepreneurs as there were non-*bumiputera* entrepreneurs.

As a step towards achieving this NEP target, the Government decided that certain companies owned fully or partially by PNB should be divested to *bumiputera* companies or individuals, considered capable of buying the necessary shares and managing the companies. It was always believed that, if a company was run by a capable *bumiputera* who had invested a substantial sum in the enterprise, the company would be better run and more profitable.

Quite obviously, the *bumiputera* purchasers of these companies had to be very carefully selected. They had to have a proven track record, which indicated their ability to manage, and a good credit rating to ensure that the banks would lend them the substantial sums of money – often in excess of RM1 billion – required to buy the blocks of shares. The best criterion for selection was their ownership of viable and profitable companies that were involved in the same kind of business as the PNB companies they proposed to acquire. Unfortunately, there were not many such *bumiputeras*, and numerous proposals from other *bumiputeras* had to be rejected. There was, of course, no guarantee that even the few selected *bumiputeras* would succeed, but so far the performance of the companies acquired by them from PNB has been quite good.

It can be shown that PNB, which caters for the vast majority of *bumiputeras*, has not lost through the sale of these shares to individual *bumiputeras*. In the first place, the shares were sold at a premium, frequently higher than the current market price, and certainly above the sum that PNB originally paid for them. PNB not only realised cash, which could be reinvested in other profitable companies, but also made capital gains. The loss of earnings from the shares of the transferred company were easily recouped through the reinvestment of the proceeds from the sale. At the same time, PNB retained a sizeable portion of the shares of the company, and there was a real possibility that, with better management and higher profitability, these remaining shares would yield almost as much as PNB had earned before the sale.

This is not to say that PNB was poor at management. On the contrary, it proved very good indeed at managing investments worth tens of billions of ringgit in a diverse range of businesses.

Most of the PNB companies were well managed, even though the involvement of PNB personnel was on the whole small, their role being more often than not in a supervisory capacity. But, due to the sheer number of companies that PNB had a stake in or owned directly, the management was spread too thinly to manage them really effectively for growth and expansion. As a result, the true potential of these companies was not realised.

The net result of the sale by PNB of its major stakes in the big Malaysian companies was to benefit the individual *bumiputera* entrepreneurs, while safeguarding the shares and profits of the more than four million unit trust holders in the Amanah Saham Nasional (ASN), the Amanah Saham Bumiputera (ASB) and later the Amanah Saham Wawasan (ASW). No one really lost anything. On the other hand, direct *bumiputera* investments and involvement in the management of large companies were enhanced, contributing to the elimination of the identification of race with economic function, this time with regard to entre-preneurship. This strategy really resulted in a 'win-win' situation.

Privatisation, as was pointed out earlier, proved an effective instrument for increasing *bumiputera* participation in all areas of business. Yet privatisation has also benefited the non-*bumi-puteras*, for they too have come forward with privatisation proposals. Their involvement has been necessary because the number of privatisation projects far exceeds the number of *bumi-putera* entrepreneurs and their agencies. Fortunately, these non-*bumiputeras* have always upheld the NEP by having *bumiputera* partners, who actively participate in their projects.

Cynics, of course, deny the fairness of the NEP. They always point to the few *bumiputera* individuals who seem to have ben-efited disproportionately from the policy. But it must be reiterated that the NEP was not about making every *bumiputera* rich, nor was it about equitable distribution amongst all the *bumiputeras*. The NEP was never concerned with the idealism of an egalitarian society, as conceived by the communist and socialist ideologists. Rather it was about balancing the opportunities and wealth between the different racial groups in Malaysia. So there had to be *bumiputeras* who became rich due to the NEP and the privatisation policy, but they were not just any *bumiputeras*. They were the obviously capable ones.

The Chinese and other non-*bumiputeras* in Malaysia experience and accept the inequity in their own communities. There are poor people, middle income people and rich people amongst them. There are hawkers, wage earners, small businessmen and company executives amongst them, just as there are highly successful and wealthy entrepreneurs.

The NEP sought from its inception to establish equity between the races and not between classes of people. The NEP was intended to desegregate the economic activities of the different communities. The Malays and the other *bumiputeras* had largely been peasant farmers, rubber tappers, smallholders and Government employees; while the Chinese and other non-*bumiputeras* were mostly townspeople, engaged in trade, commerce and the professions. If the *bumiputeras* and non-*bumiputeras* were mixed in the rural and urban areas, and involved in similar economic and other activities, then racial differences would not be amplified by economic disparities. In other words, the *bumiputeras* would no longer be associated with the poverty and backwardness of the rural peasantry, starkly contrasted by the wealth and urban sophistication of the non-*bumiputeras*.

The mere disparity between the rich and poor is often enough on its own a cause of bitterness, envy and conflict, sometimes accompanied by violence. Of course, it was this economic disparity within the same ethnic group which communism and socialism were supposed to eradicate. In practice, however, the ideal of a classless society has proved impossible to achieve. When economic disparity is exacerbated by racial division, the potential for conflict is even greater. Such was the case in Malaysia. The *bumiputeras* were not only *bumiputeras* but also poor, while the non-*bumiputeras* were not only ethnically different but also richer.

The NEP's ideal was a nation in which there would still be different classes, but where each class would be composed of people from the different racial groups, in roughly the same proportion as each race makes up the overall population of Malaysia. In this way the *bumiputeras* would not just see themselves as *bumiputeras*, but also identify themselves with non-*bumiputeras* of the same class.

The NEP has been able to achieve, at least partly, the objective of removing the identification of race with economic function. But the proportions are still not right. There remain more rich non-*bumiputeras* than rich *bumiputeras*, and there are more middle-class non-*bumiputeras*. On the other hand, there are rather more poor *bumiputeras* than poor non-*bumiputeras*.

While Malaysia's towns are no longer the preserve of the non-*bumiputeras*, the number of *bumiputeras* and their businesses remains rather small. There is now, however, a far greater equity of risk in the urban areas. If any catastrophe, man-made or natural, were to hit the towns, *bumiputeras* would also be affected. In the May 1969 troubles, when the Malays rioted in Kuala Lumpur, burning buildings and cars, they were certain that this property belonged to the non-*bumiputeras*. Today, if they were to riot in Kuala Lumpur and the other towns of Malaysia and damage property, they could well be damaging property belonging to *bumiputeras*.

There is a growing *bumiputera* middle class, but the proportion is again not right. Most of the middle-class housing estates are owned and occupied by non-*bumiputeras*. To a certain extent, this is due to the *bumiputeras* preferring to live where their numbers are concentrated, even if they do not form a majority. But, despite concessionary prices, there are insufficient numbers of *bumiputeras* who can afford to purchase medium-price properties. This militates against the kind of racial mix which the NEP was supposed to bring about. Equity has not been achieved in terms of housing.

While the objective of the NEP to eliminate the identification of race with economic function has been the focus of attention and controversy, the achievement of the other objective, poverty eradication, without discrimination as to race, has been largely ignored. Yet this objective was as important to the NEP as balancing the economic development between the different races. Indeed, poverty eradication was a part of the same balancing act, the objective being to ensure that all the different races were equally free from poverty.

In the developed countries of the West, the approach to poverty eradication is based almost exclusively on subsidies and aid. The whole panoply of the welfare state – unemployment benefit or the dole, old-age pensions, free medical treatment and other social security payments – is designed to help relieve poverty. If these benefits were withdrawn, the degree and extent of poverty in the developed countries of the West would be worse than in the developing countries. Today, in many developed countries, more than 10% of the workforce is unemployed. Without the dole, the unemployed would be the majority of poor people in the community. During the Great Depression of the 1930s, unemployment reached unprecedented levels in the West: 14 million in the USA, 6 million in Germany and 3 million in the UK. With welfare systems at an embryonic stage or just non-existent, unemployment resulted in poverty and real hardship.

There may be some justification for handing out public money to the poor, so as to give them a 'decent' living. Yet there have been numerous cases, often highly publicised, where the dole paid to individuals actually made them better off than many employed people. The unemployment benefit in these instances was often calculated as a percentage of the so-called normal income of the person concerned. Somebody used to drawing an income many times greater than the average worker would be paid as much as 90% of his or her normal earnings. This is an obvious abuse of social justice. The poverty line seems to be irregular: higher for the high income earners and lower for the low income earners. Thus even amongst the unemployed some are richer than others, or, alternatively, some are poorer than other equally unemployed people. Basic inequalities are thus perpetuated, even while living on public charity. The rich remain richer than the poor even in 'poverty'. It is strange that this distorted perception of right and wrong should gain acceptance at all in the so-called civilised West.

Government support and charity are the last resort in dealing with poverty in Malaysia. The real responsibility for the poor lies with the family, and sometimes the extended family. They must care for the poor members of their family and their relatives. It will be a strain on many of them, but this will encourage the unemployed family member to seek a job quickly. Of course, some may not be able to extend meaningful support, as they are themselves very poor. In such cases, and such cases only, the Government provides aid. Funds are allocated to build a small, sub-standard dwelling, in addition to some allowance for basic needs. Very few Malaysians really fall into this category, as most people have some relatives willing to support destitute members of the family.

In a celebrated case which led to student demonstrations in 1974, a child was alleged to have died of poverty. The family was said to be starving and the child had died from malnutrition. The mother had passed away and the three children were being brought up by their father. Welfare officers investigated the case and found sufficient stocks of rice and other foodstuffs in the family home. The father felt insulted by the widespread belief that he had allowed his child to starve to death when he had plenty of food in the house. The child had in fact died from an unrelated illness.

The family was from a *kampung*, or village. Under no circumstances would the villagers have allowed anybody from their *kampung* to die from starvation. Whatever little food was available would have been shared with any villager so poor as to have no food. There was in fact no one starving in the village. The culture of Malaysian rural society is such that it is impossible for anyone to starve to death. Moreover, there has never been famine and consequent starvation in Malaysia. The land is so fertile that it requires little effort to grow food for personal consumption.

This does not mean that the Government ignores people stricken by a very rare drought or other natural catastrophe which may affect the country. The Government has always provided food supplies, drinking water or disaster relief when these have been needed. But for poverty the preference is to provide the opportunity for gainful employment, rather than to give unemployment benefit. There are, for example, subsidy schemes for *padi* farmers. But these are not meant to combat poverty. They are intended to keep the price of *padi* under control, so that the rest of the population is not burdened by continuously inflated prices for their staple food. Fishermen also receive similar subsidies to control the price of fish.

The principal strategy for poverty eradication amongst all racial groups under the NEP was the creation of jobs. The Government established favourable conditions and provided incentives for an expansion of the workforce, with a marked emphasis on growth in labour-intensive industries during the Second and Third Malaysia Plans (1971–5 and 1976–80). Many potential investors in Malaysia, particularly foreign industrialists, were looking to reduce their production costs to make them more competitive in world markets. Malaysia offered them an effective means to achieve this reduction, with its low-cost labour force. Attracted by this, investors set up labour-intensive industries which quickly brought full employment to Malaysia. In the process, poverty was also reduced.

But low wages may result in relative poverty. To minimise this risk, the Government tried to ensure that inflation remained low. In Malaysia inflation has been less than 4% almost since independence. The fourfold increases in world oil prices in 1974 caused the inflation rate to leap to 17%, which could have been disastrous if the Government had not moved quickly to reduce the rate to a reasonable level. With inflation often hitting over 100% in some developing countries, Malaysia's inflation rate must be considered very low indeed.

Low inflation resulted in a slower increase in wages, thus attracting more and more investment, leading to the creation of even more jobs. Of course, the demand for labour itself resulted in upward pressure on wages. This helped to reduce relative poverty. Wages today in Malaysia are much higher than when the NEP was launched. But what is important is that purchasing power has also increased because inflation has remained low, i.e. real incomes have risen. Many countries may have more rapid increases in income levels, but they are rendered meaningless in real terms because of high inflation rates.

The incidence of absolute poverty was reduced from 49.3% to 16.5% during the period of the NEP, and is now only 8.9%. In any society there will be intractable poverty cases, but in Malaysia the number is the lowest possible. As has been pointed out, the incidence of poverty would be much greater in the developed countries of the West than in Malaysia if unemployment benefit were discounted. On the other hand, if the Government's minimal aid and help from the family were taken into account, there would be no poverty in Malaysia. Certainly, no one starves to death in Malaysia, and neither do people have to resort to foraging in rubbish heaps, as happens in a number of countries.

It may be argued that unemployment benefit is a means of redistributing wealth, or it is a regulated way of making families contribute through taxation, along with everybody else, to maintaining the poorer members of their family. But this is not the same. When support is made mandatory and is provided by a government agency, family links will be broken. The government can 'dole' out money, but it cannot give the kind of love provided by family members, especially in the case of the elderly and infirm. Moreover, when the poor are assured of being taken care of rather generously by the government, there will be little incentive for them to work and earn a living. Certainly, they will not work for less than they can get from the dole. The result is voluntary unemployment.

There are now moves in many western developed countries to give those on unemployment benefit manual work to do. But, as was to be expected, the trade unions are protesting against such schemes. For the unions, general unemployment is not their concern. The government bears responsibility for taking care of the unemployed. The unions are concerned only with the working conditions and ever increasing wages of their members. They are not interested in poverty eradication.

Everything was fine when the developed West monopolised world markets. Whenever wages rose, the price of the goods produced also rose, while the purchase price of the raw materials, usually imported from developing countries, was pushed down. But when some developing countries, including Malaysia, began to produce the same goods and invaded the world markets, the high wages in the West could not be sustained.

The solution should have been to lower wages. But wages, once they have gone up in the West, can never come down. The trade unions will not allow it. They would rather bankrupt their industries than reduce their members' wages. The result was the closure of industries and a reduction in the number of jobs, and indeed in union membership, as well as the loss of new job-creating investments.

The jobless in the West are entitled to unemployment benefit. The funds for this must come from taxes on industry and business, as well as the incomes of those still working. However, as company closures and unemployment increase, tax revenue must inevitably decrease. At the same time, the number of unemployed people needing government support increases. In short, government revenue falls just when welfare payments are rising rapidly. If the government resorts to raising taxation, industry and business become even less profitable and this may result in further closures, throwing yet more workers out of a job and on the dole.

When the idea of unemployment benefits was first conceived

in Germany and Britain at the end of the 19th century, it was assumed there would always be sufficient revenue from taxation on thriving businesses to support the unemployed at a decent standard of living. Indeed, the prevailing opinion was that their lifestyles should not change at all. The unemployed were to be given a level of benefit almost as high as the wages they had received when they were working.

But why should people work when there is hardly any difference in their incomes and lifestyles, whether they are employed or unemployed? As more and more people choose not to work, or companies dismiss workers at the slightest economic downturn, knowing that the government will take care of them, the number of people working and businesses operating will decline, reducing the amount of taxes collectable. Again the result will be that government revenue falls at the same time as more funds are needed to pay unemployment benefit.

The western system of unemployment benefit may seem to reflect the values of a caring government and society. But actually it reflects the uncaring attitude of the family and the people. The idea that the state is a better provider is erroneous. The government can raise money to care for the unemployed and the unemployable only by taxing the employed, whether directly or indirectly. The money still comes from the same people, who do not like spending their money on their destitute relatives. They still have to pay. But the care is at most second best and bereft of love.

In the process, unemployment benefit or the dole destroys the family. Perhaps the concepts of family life, and family love and responsibility, are out of date. They are certainly declining in the West. The extended family network has been destroyed, and now even the nuclear family is under threat. This is seen in the temporary cohabitation of two or more people, on occasion of the same sex, sometimes with their own offspring. It is also seen in the proliferation of single-parent families, the legacy of a sexual liberation dating from the 1960s and a soaring divorce rate. In these circumstances, the children from such families cannot be expected to value family life. Rather they perpetuate the non-family system and the kind of morals or lack of morals which go with it. They too will disdain marriage, cohabiting heterosexually or homosexually.

This is not the kind of society that Malaysia wants. We want to retain the family, even the extended family. Unemployment benefit and the dole system must be considered family breakers. We would rather pay more to the employed, if we can afford to, than pay unemployment benefit. With the employed earning more, they would be better able to look after the unemployed and unemployable members of their families.

The method chosen by the Government to eradicate poverty, as implemented under the NEP, was to stimulate the creation of jobs, so that everyone who wanted to be employed would be able to work, and earn a wage commensurate with the nature of their job. With this objective in mind, foreign and domestic investors were encouraged, initially in key labour-intensive industries. When full employment was achieved, the Government tried to ensure that wages went up in line with productivity and without any pressure from the workers through strikes and the like, as these tend to reduce investment and job creation, leading to unemployment and poverty.

This strategy worked very well for Malaysia. Today, there is statistically no unemployment. This alone has resulted in the eradication of absolute poverty. There is, of course, relative poverty, since some people must earn less than the average. There is also statistical poverty due to some people not wanting to work, or being unable to work. The disabled and the destitute who have no family to support them are given only minimal Government aid.

There are some two million foreign workers in Malaysia, who are largely gainfully employed. For a country with a population of 20 million, the proportion of foreign workers is bigger than that found in most developed countries. Some of these workers earn very high wages. Some are still looking for jobs. The latter create the picture of urban poverty seen in Malaysia. But their presence does indicate that Malaysians who wish to work should be able to find employment, and free themselves from poverty.

The NEP's first objective was to eradicate poverty irrespective of race. By any measure, this has been achieved. Moreover, it has been achieved in a positive fashion, without the creation of make-believe jobs as in the communist countries, and without any disruption to the Malaysian economy.

With the eradication of poverty and the elimination of the identification of race with economic function largely achieved, the NEP objectives must be considered as having been successfully implemented. Since the NEP was dependent on economic growth, and enviable levels of growth have indeed taken place, the equity objective has clearly not been achieved at the expense of growth, as many had originally predicted. In fact the growth during the NEP period was exceptionally high, averaging almost 7%. Few countries have achieved such sustained rates of growth, even without being saddled with a need to achieve equity between different groups, whether social or ethnic. But Malaysia has achieved growth with equity.

By combining racial equity with economic growth, Malaysia has managed to remain politically stable and have harmonious relations between the different ethnic groups. This is a fact that few can challenge. The critics have been proved wrong. They will continue to deride the NEP and harp about the discrimination involved. But Malaysia can confidently ignore them. The policy, modified to suit the prevailing political and economic situation, will continue to be implemented until the *bumiputeras* and the non-*bumiputeras* lose their fear of each other and achieve the true unity of *Bangsa Malaysia*, or a fully united and ethnically integrated Malaysian nation, living in harmony, and full and fair partnership. That is the ultimate aim of the NEP and its successor, the National Development Policy (NDP).

5

The Cultural Dimension

... and Melaka became a great city. Strangers flocked thither ... and from below the wind to above the wind Melaka became famous as a very great city ... so much so that princes from all countries came to present themselves before [the] sultan ..., who treated them with due respect bestowing upon them robes of honour and of the highest distinction together with rich presents of jewels, gold and silver.

The Malay Annals (early 17th century)

A S THE NAME implies, the New Economic Policy (NEP) was about economic matters; to be exact, about restructuring the Malaysian economy so that the different races who make up the population would each have a fair share of the nation's economic wealth. This was not to be achieved by redistributing existing wealth, through expropriating what belonged to the wealthy and then sharing it equitably amongst the rest. Instead, the restructuring was to be achieved through creating new wealth, and giving the opportunities for acquiring such wealth disproportionately, so that the 'have-nots' would have more opportunities than the 'haves'.

The onus was therefore not just on the Government to create and apportion opportunities for the acquisition of wealth by the *bumiputeras*, but also on the *bumiputeras* themselves to know how to use these opportunities, in order to translate them into wealth. Simply put, the Government would issue contracts or exclusive business licences to the *bumiputeras*, but from then on the *bumiputeras* had to manage and develop their own economic growth.

But the *bumiputeras* were largely peasant farmers or petty traders and hawkers. Mere opportunity, or even the provision of adequate facilities such as credit and premises, would not ensure the business success of these farmers and petty traders. To succeed, they needed management skills of the superior quality possessed by the non-*bumiputeras*. In fact, a major cultural change was required, a leap over the chasm which separated the culture of the peasant and petty trader from that of a sophisticated commercial community.

Why did there have to be a cultural change? The answer was that the performance of any community or race is basically a reflection of the value system of that particular people, which forms the basis of their culture. Ethnic differences are not a determinant of the cultural outlook or sophistication of a particular race. Tribes or nations with distinctly different levels of cultural development or civilisation may come from the same ethnic group. One group may be very successful, while another may fail in every field of human endeavour. The reason lies in the value system each group develops. A culture compatible with success will succeed, but one that is not compatible will fail.

A people's culture, rooted in the sum total of the values believed in by that community, is truly the determinant of their performance in any activity. Culturally unsophisticated and commercially backward farmers and petty traders cannot reasonably be expected to succeed in commerce and industry, simply because they are given the opportunity. For the NEP to succeed, it was therefore essential that the *bumiputera* peasants and petty traders acquire the value systems and sophistication of a complex commercial and industrial community.

The failure of the NEP in the early days could be traced to the lack of attention given to inculcating the right culture amongst the *bumiputeras*. When shares and licences were indiscriminately distributed to them, they merely sold them off to the non-*bumiputeras*, in order to achieve quick wealth. As they were not familiar with or able to manage wealth, the easy gains were soon dissipated and they became poor again. If this had been allowed to go on, even in a thousand years the *bumiputeras* would still have been poor, while the non-*bumiputeras* would have become richer and richer from managing what they had reacquired from the *bumiputeras*. But the NEP was to last only twenty years. Without acquiring a new culture, the NEP target for the *bumiputeras* would not be achieved.

BUMIPUTERA CULTURE IN THE PAST

The peasantry, born and bred in the countryside, have always understood land as a source of wealth. It is nature's bounty. For a minimal input of physical labour, land can yield a fair amount of income. To generate more wealth, the only requirement is more land. Admittedly, some farming communities achieve a fair degree of sophistication. They choose the right crops, introduce irrigation schemes, and use technology in the form of fertilisers and mechanisation, so as to improve crop yield. The ancient Egyptians built one of the world's great civilisations, symbolised by the pyramids, through their agricultural sophistication in exploiting the resources of the Nile valley.

Unfortunately, the peasant farmers of Malaysia never developed a high level of agricultural sophistication. They did not even understand the more complex uses of money. Money was a convenience, used as a substitute for goods in bartering. Money as capital was not appreciated. Many Malay farmers agreed to surrender their next harvest to the local Chinese shop-keeper or rice mill-owner, as an advance to meet their daily needs and the requirements of the next planting season. Most of them were so naive that they did not ask for accounts to be kept of the value of their harvest or of the goods they had taken. They were happy to be able to draw whatever money or goods they needed from the shopkeeper or the mill-owner. Whether they had over-drawn or underdrawn seemed unimportant to them. Nor did they care whether any interest had been earned. As Muslims, the Malays did not care for interest anyway. What mattered was that they had easy access to money and goods.

Clearly, the management of money was not a skill the Malay peasants had mastered. Their children of today may be better educated, but this does not mean they fully appreciate the role and value of money in commerce. For a long time, the only way they knew how to acquire capital for business was through savings. Alternatively, they expected relatives or friends to lend them capital on an interest-free basis. Repayment of such loans was not regarded as an obligation. Neither were the lenders too insistent on repayment. Naturally, large capital sums could not be raised for any major agricultural or commercial venture.

This lackadaisical attitude towards credit has never really disappeared. Thus loans given by the Majlis Amanah Rakyat (MARA) for studying and business purposes are often not repaid, even when the borrowers have the means to pay. While they may not know it, this attitude towards the repayment of loans is a part of the historic *bumiputera* culture. Such an attitude is not conducive to business. Banks will certainly not lend unless they are sure of being repaid. Since far too many *bumiputeras* tend to renege on the repayment of their debts, they generally find difficulty even now in raising loans. No business can really grow on internally generated funds alone. If credit becomes difficult to obtain, *bumiputera* businesses cannot grow. Yet the NEP was dependent on growth and new wealth.

Unable to appreciate the role of money, careless about accounting and even more so about the repayment of debts, the ability of the *bumiputeras* to seize the opportunities created for them by the NEP in the commercial world appeared initially quite small. In other words, it seemed that the objective of the NEP to eliminate the identification of race with economic function could not be realised.

In Sarawak and Sabah there was also the problem of communal landholdings. This was a useful mechanism for ensuring that native land did not pass into the hands of non-natives. But managing communal land was very difficult, as virtually everyone had to be consulted before anything could be done to develop the land. It often proved impossible to reach a consensus, particularly when, due to a lack of capital or know-how, non-natives needed to be involved in the proposed project. As a result, native land usually remained neglected and of low economic value. Since the communal owners could not develop their land themselves, they never acquired the skills and experience of management. Without such skills, they could not make a success of the opportunities created by the NEP, designed to bring them into the mainstream of the country's economic life. Here was another barrier to the NEP, a barrier that could be overcome only by changing the value system, so that land ownership was not regarded as being equally important as the wealth that could be extracted from it. The peasant mentality was far too much influenced by merely owning land, rather than regarding it as an asset for the creation of more wealth.

Although there was no communal land ownership in the Malay Peninsula, much of the land was designated Malay reserve land, or native customary land. Once again, the intention was to prevent ownership of land from passing out of *bumiputera* hands.

The market value of land depends on what the market can afford. If the community is rich, the value will be high, and vice versa. Since the Malays were poorer than the Chinese, Malay reserve land had a lower value than non-*bumiputera* land. This low value was further reduced as the banks were not allowed to accept Malay reserve land as collateral. Thus obtaining loan capital for business became almost impossible. Protected by the Malay land reserve laws, a culture of dependence developed amongst the Malays. They might be poor in financial terms, but they had land, and land ownership symbolised their right to the country, their 'special' position as *bumiputeras*, or 'sons of the soil'. If this state of affairs was allowed to continue, Malay wealth would remain only symbolic and not real.

Growth is a phenomenon which usually accompanies business activities. Even farmers can experience growth, if they know how to manage the proceeds from their farming activities. They can purchase additional land, buy new farm machinery to take advantage of more efficient agricultural techniques, or even invest outside the farming sector. But peasant farmers almost always live from hand to mouth, remaining at a subsistence level, experiencing no growth at all. Worse still, the share of the land diminishes with each passing generation when the land is divided between the offspring. As there is no principle of primogeniture in Muslim inheritance laws, Malay farmers could only get poorer and poorer. One of the reasons for introducing the pioneer land schemes under the Federal Land Development Agency (FELDA) and Federal Land Consolidation and Rehabilitation Authority (FELCRA), was the need to make new land available to the impoverished offspring of Malay farmers. But land in Malaysia is not unlimited. The land distribution approach to poverty eradication could not have gone on indefinitely.

There were some *bumiputeras* who did not own land and were therefore unable to make a living from farming. They invariably turned to petty trading and hawking. These small businesses were by implication owner-operated. No shareholders were involved. Capital was tiny and, in many instances, monetary capital was not involved. This was the case when the individual concerned simply collected products from the jungle, or created handcrafted goods from freely available raw materials.

When such an individual was responsible only to himself for his working activities, he seldom adopted a responsible attitude. Petty traders and hawkers saw no necessity in keeping accounts, or even finding out whether they had made a profit or not. They often considered that 100% of the proceeds of a sale constituted profit, not being too careful about deducting costs, or, for that matter, setting aside profits for future investment or expansion. They did not feel the need to provide for a rainy day, and would be happy if they made enough for their daily needs. They did not think of trying to reinvest in order to make more.

While a handful of petty traders and hawkers went on to become successful businessmen largely through personal initiative, the culture of the petty trader and hawker was such that their outlook was not compatible with the demands of big business, with its different management systems and needs. They were not acquainted with accounting procedures, banking practices, the management of staff, the notion of growth and the complex overhead costs of a large commercial set-up. It was not that they did not want to be successful, to grow and to be wealthy. It was just that their petty trading and hawking culture did not prepare them for modern business in a sophisticated mercantile and industrial society.

Work ethics play a very big role in the success of any enterprise. If nothing else, hard work is a prerequisite for mastering and managing the ever more complex structure of a business organisation, where the emphasis is not just on managing business in accordance with accepted practices, but, more importantly, on dealing with people who are involved directly or indirectly with the company. It is simple when a company is capitalised, managed and owned by a single individual. He is responsible to and for himself only. He will not have to satisfy and interact with others, including partners, executives, bankers, shareholders and employees. What a one-man petty trader or hawker does is truly his own business.

It is possible to set up a big private company entirely owned by a single individual. But, as part of a big organisation concerned with commerce and industry, one's business is no longer truly one's own, even if it is privately owned or a proprietorship. There will always be numerous people to interact with: for instance, loans to be raised, which involves winning the confidence of the lenders. Sooner or later, if the business is to expand, public capital and shares will be needed. The management of the company will then be a different ball game.

Ethics become extremely important when managing a company that is not entirely owned by the businessman himself. Managing other people's capital requires integrity and accountability. No longer can one 'borrow' the company's money or use any of the company's staff or facilities on a whim or a fancy. A proper set of ethical business practices will have to be an integral part of the culture.

All of this requires certain attitudes and approaches, for which the peasant farmer and the petty trader were ill-equipped. Their culture was totally different, and, unless this culture was radically changed, there was no possibility of transforming a peasant and petty trading community into a modern business one. Yet this was essential for the achievement of the NEP's objectives.

Even civil servants, who constituted a fair proportion of the *bumiputera* community, do not necessarily make good businessmen. Their culture was, and still is, different from that of the business world. Civil servants and other public sector employees are mainly involved in collecting taxes and spending government money. But managing government finances is not the same as managing company money for profit, where fixing prices in order to be competitive, while at the same time making a reasonable return, is all important. The money managed by civil servants is not their own and, consequently, they have a more relaxed attitude about how it is being used.

Poor management of government funds can result in losses, but such losses are often accepted and even excused. Governments frequently have budget deficits for years on end, without worrying too much about the excess of expenditure over income. Funds can always be borrowed, raised through tax increases, or received as aid from richer countries. It is exceptional for a government to care overly for the good management of revenue and expenditure. This casual approach to financial affairs is all too often imbibed by the civil servants.

Civil servants, and in particular those at the executive level, are generally highly educated and very able. While their culture is not fully compatible with the world of business, they would in all likelihood need less time to switch to business and develop a new culture than farmers and petty traders. Their chances of success would, of course, be greater. But it was never certain that they could make the transformation successfully and prosper in business. If the civil servants amongst the *bumiputeras* could not be relied upon to succeed in business, the achievement of the NEP objectives seemed very unlikely.

NEW ETHICS AND BUSINESS PRACTICES

The NEP was about changing the *bumiputeras* from a farming, petty trading and civil service community to one that was commercial and industrial, comparable in size and wealth to the commercial and industrial non-*bumiputera* community. Such a change could not be effected unless a cultural transformation, or revolution, took place prior to or during the process.

There is a parallel here with the cultural change currently taking place amongst the people of central and eastern Europe, as their countries move from centrally planned, communist economies to free market, capitalist ones. At the start, they not only lacked capital, and entrepreneurial and management skills, but their cultural values, originating from the ideals of Marx and Engels, and given greater definition by Stalin's Five Year Plans in the Soviet Union, were also very different. They were used to sinecure low-paid employment in a subsidised and state-owned economy. Profits and losses were of no concern to anyone, whether managers or workers. A dependence mentality prevailed which undermined work ethics, resulting in a culture based on the belief that the state had the responsibility to provide everything for everyone from 'cradle to grave'.

With the sudden adoption of free market practices after 1989, these people had to learn almost overnight the value of money and the meaning of the bottom line. They found it very difficult adjusting to this new culture, even understanding it. The governments also found it difficult, having to transfer monopolistic state services and supply functions to private individuals. Frequently, these individuals failed too. In simple terms, the communist culture was just not compatible with the rough and tumble and competitive atmosphere of the market place. It was often the less acceptable elements in society, such as those involved in organised crime, who responded best to the new capitalist challenge. The clumsy and chronically inefficient administrative procedures of communism were simply an anachronism in a commercial world of highly efficient management techniques, where the bottom line was profits and growth.

To change the *bumiputeras* from farmers, petty traders and public servants to businessmen was just as difficult. Unless they went through a cultural revolution of the right kind, they would fail, and if they failed, the NEP would fail too. The Government had to oversee and manage the change from the extant *bumiputera* culture to one that was compatible with the running of businesses at all levels.

This cultural change was achieved, in the process making a major contribution to the success of the NEP. How was this accomplished? The simple answer is by precept and example. The *bumiputeras*, especially the leaders of the Government and related agencies, had to acquire and practise new work ethics. They had to learn discipline and the meaning of hard work. 'Leadership by example' was made the motto of the Government. If example was to be used effectively, the leaders had to change first and demonstrate the new culture in the course of their work. They had also to disseminate the new culture.

Seminars, courses and training camps were used to inculcate new values and perceptions, in accordance with a culture compatible with involvement in trade, business and the market place. Some *bumiputeras* with the potential to go a long way in business attended work camps, where new value systems were explained and spread, along with the reasoning behind the NEP and the factors necessary for its success. Millions of ringgit were spent on propagating and instilling a new set of values, in order to create a new *bumiputera* culture.

While it might have been prudent to expose the *bumiputeras* gradually to modern business, the NEP time-frame of twenty years demanded a rapid cultural transformation. Certain *bumiputeras* were therefore allowed, or even encouraged, to acquire rapidly the new ethics and work culture. This was not, however, the best way to instil new values. Some moved up too fast and found themselves out of their depth. They failed, but quite a few did make it. Today, *bumiputera* big business is managed effectively by *bumiputera* entrepreneurs and managers, whose skills and business knowledge are second to none. These people have apparently acquired and mastered the new culture.

Cultural change creates its own momentum. The important thing is to set it in motion, and to achieve a good start. The people initiating the change must not only understand the problem and the areas needing change, but also define the new culture and its values.

To effect a change in culture is a complex, intricate and extensive matter. There is no single factor which, after change, will miraculously bring about the required results. A whole range of changes have to be made, which in effect create virtually a new people. Culture is, of course, what distinguishes people, not ethnicity or nationality. Changing the culture means changing the characteristics of a people which had previously distinguished them, to a different set of characteristics which will become identified with the new culture and therefore the 'new' people.

In fact, cultural change never ceases. The people of today may be the descendants of people of the past, but culturally they are hardly the same. The differences can be very striking. The British of the prudish, if somewhat hypocritical, Victorian era are very different from their descendants of today. Yet they are still recognisable as the British. The same applies to almost all the various races and nationalities of the world. Ongoing cultural changes may be insignificant or they may be radical, but change is constant, whether it happens consciously or unconsciously.

The cultural change which the Malays and the other *bumiputeras* underwent has made them very different from their predecessors, but they are still Malays, Ibans, Kadazans and so on. Many of the distinguishing features of the various *bumiputera* groups remain. They still speak the same languages, albeit laced with new words, and preserve their indigenous skills and arts, albeit in a more modern fashion. But as far as their business culture is concerned, they have changed almost completely. They are almost a totally different people.

One of the most important aspects of *bumiputera* culture which changed, deliberately as well as incidentally, was self-confidence. The Malays and the other *bumiputeras* had little confidence in their own abilities. Having lived under British colonial rule and having been separated from the aggressively successful immigrant races, the *bumiputeras* were convinced that they could never succeed as other peoples had succeeded. They believed they were not as good or as capable as others, and felt they needed support all the time, indeed for ever. They felt a need to be held by the hand and led.

This lack of self-confidence was incompatible not only with business success, but also with any meaningful cultural change. Only people confident of themselves are willing to try new approaches and ideas, and, perhaps most important of all, to do so with a high expectation of success. Cultural change is not only about trying new things, but also about trying something which may be irreversible, and it takes real confidence to try something which cannot be reversed.

A 'can do' philosophy had to be introduced. The *bumiputeras* had to believe they were capable of doing everything that others could do, and that they could do these things well. An image of success had to be created through the use of role models, as nothing would be more persuasive than seeing other *bumiputeras* succeeding in life. These role models might seem to be privileged and dedicated to self alone, but their success in Malaysia was pivotal to the progress of the *bumiputeras*. They helped convince them that cultural change was possible and by implication that the NEP could be a success.

The NEP was therefore as much a reform strategy as it was an attempt to correct the economic injustices found in multiracial Malaysia. Success could not only be limited to the correction of the perceived discrimination, inequity and injustice in the social and economic border of the country. The NEP had to be encouraged and made permanent by the restructuring of *bumiputera* culture.

Such a revolution would obviously take time. Yet, as the NEP was limited to only twenty years, the beginnings at least of the revolution had to be achieved during that period. The culture of the peasant farmer, the petty trader and hawker, and the wage earner had to be replaced by the deliberate cultivation of the culture of a commercial and industrial society of the most modern kind. Central to this was the attitude towards finance. Money had to be regarded no longer as a mere convenience, but as capital for investment and an instrument for the creation of wealth through the complex transactions involved in modern business and trade.

A cultural change may not necessarily be good; it can in fact be thoroughly bad, or a change for the good may be accompanied by one that is bad. A culture compatible with big business can be suitable for organised crime. It may result in extreme materialism and avarice. It may be associated with fraud on a grand scale.

The cultural change needed to make the NEP a success did indeed result in cases of criminal acquisitiveness and the misuse of wealth. There has undoubtedly been an increase in embezzlement, bribery, breaches of trust, money politics and greed. But this must not result in faint hearts, or any attempt to return to the old ways and a culture of poverty. There is no virtue in being poor. Neither is there any guarantee that poverty will not be accompanied by crime and misdemeanours. The scale may be smaller, but, relative to the capacity of the poor, the degree will be just as high. In Malaysia, poverty amongst the *bumiputeras*, alongside wealth confined to the non-*bumiputeras*, would have had even worse consequences than mere crimes and corruption. It is not that we must excuse the accompanying ills. We must try and prevent them from occurring. But they must not deflect us from our promotion of continued cultural change for the long-term success of the NEP.

The solution lies in eliminating what seem to be the less savoury side-effects of the culture of wealth and the management skills required to attain it. This may not be totally successful, but no culture from any period in history, even those divinely inspired, has been able to banish completely evil and criminal abuses. The important thing is that society makes every effort to deal seriously with these unfortunate side-effects.

Just as the new culture for the *bumiputeras* has been deliberately implanted and developed, so the elimination of the abuses must be carefully planned and executed. This can again be done by precept and example. At the same time, the right dose of punishment for abuses should act as a deterrent; punishment which must be enforced seriously and consistently.

THE EVOLUTION OF CULTURAL VALUES

Throughout the history of mankind, attempts have been made to improve the quality of life. Man made his initial improvements by adjusting to his surroundings and environment. The first shelters were natural, with caves being a familiar habitat for early man. Advancing from this primitive stage, man began to shape his surroundings to suit his needs. He constructed shelters for himself and his family. This process of shaping the environment to suit the needs and aspirations of man has never ceased. The cities, houses, flats and 'intelligent' buildings of today are nothing more than a highly sophisticated refinement of man's first crude lean-to shelters of branches and leaves.

The status or the stage of a community's evolution can be gauged from the nature of the shelters it develops. These range from the minimal adjustments made by man to his immediate environment to suit his needs, to the modern cities of the world, with their complex infrastructure and buildings.

Steps leading up to a wooden house built on stilts can be

hacked from a single tree trunk. This is an obvious attempt to make entering the house easier by adapting the immediate surroundings to a human use, although the user would still have to possess a degree of agility to climb such primitive stairs. Of course, they are not meant for patent leather shoes with smooth soles! The feet should be bare and quite prehensile if the stairs are to be climbed with ease. In time, not only will those living in the house acquire the necessary agility, but even the shape and callosity of their feet will develop according to the requirements of climbing the stairs. The escalator is the modern equivalent of the steps hacked from a single tree trunk. So, at a very basic level, one can deduce the stage of human development in a particular society by observing the type of staircase used.

What is worth noting is that some communities or societies seem easily satisfied, and will make no attempt to progress further. Other communities keep on striving to improve on the improvement. The latter are never satisfied with what they have achieved, and continually try to progress through observation and innovation, which in themselves become part of their civilisation and culture. The former stagnate and become progressively inferior, and are dominated by the superior and continuously advancing communities. But a stagnant society need not remain stagnant for ever. If the people realise and acknowledge their backwardness, and understand that their inferiority is due to an inherent cultural unwillingness to seek improvement, they can change some of their cultural values and progress.

There is no need for anyone to reinvent the wheel. The stagnant society can observe, learn and adopt the methods and institutions of the successful, vibrant society. The potential of the people in a stagnant society can be demonstrated by the skills they have developed in practices indigenous to their society. Many so-called primitive people excel in skills which could not easily be mastered by members of an advanced society. The talent of the *orang asli* in Peninsular Malaysia at using a blowpipe would certainly be difficult to acquire, even for hunters skilled in the use of high-powered rifles. If the *orang asli* were taught to hunt with rifles from childhood through several generations, it is not unthinkable that they would become as proficient with rifles as they are now with their blowpipes.

Clearly, the capacity to acquire new skills is a human attribute. It only needs the opportunity and constant practice. The process may take a long time, possibly even several generations, but the skills will eventually be acquired. Nor is it a process limited only to manual skills. Even the capacity to think and reason, and to resolve problems, can be developed in any people, if the opportunity and perseverance are there.

This short digression on the evolution of civilisation and culture is relevant to the problem of changing the culture of the Malays and the other *bumiputeras* in order for the NEP to be a success. Culture is a very complex matter. Apart from values, language and the arts, there are many other aspects of life which contribute to the culture of any community, race or nation. Some of the distinguishing features of a particular culture are quite difficult to identify and differentiate, but they give a distinctive flavour and character to the race or nation concerned, and may determine the people's level of achievements.

Generally, the culture of a race or nation develops naturally and unconsciously, being predominantly influenced and shaped by the environment and the emotional make-up of the people concerned. If this leads to progress, a degree of sophistication and the desire for further improvement, there may follow a deliberate effort to propagate and foster changes in the culture. Such an effort is usually determined by perceived inequities or the deleterious effect of the existing culture on the society in general, or particular elements within it.

Sometimes cultural change is divinely inspired. The great religions of the world emerged in this way. At other times, perceived injustices in a particular society result in politico-cultural change, all too often accompanied by violence. The best and most cited examples are the French and Russian revolutions.

Although the objectives in such movements were overwhelmingly political, their novelty and the scale of support they often engendered inevitably affected the culture of the people. Both France and Russia were never the same again after 1789 and 1917 respectively. The perceived injustices were corrected, but over the years the revolutionary movements themselves underwent profound change, not always for the better. The later revolutionaries were often rather different in outlook from the original pioneers. While communism was intended to bring the people material equality, the reality was rather different, undermining work ethics and competitive spirit. In the end, there was only equality of poverty and not equality of wealth.

Once a culture is developed and accepted, changing it even for the better becomes difficult. Attempts in the past have resulted in charges of heresy. In medieval Europe, the Christian church in Rome imposed a cultural uniformity, based on its teachings. Any breaches in accepted doctrine and behaviour were deemed heresy, and were subject to the prosecution of the Inquisition. Very severe punishments were usually meted out. It took many centuries and much suffering before heresy finally broke the resistance of Rome. A new dynamic Protestant culture emerged in many parts of western Europe, including Britain and Holland, a culture which in the next two hundred and fifty years formed the basis for dramatic commercial expansion, imperialism and the industrial revolution. Cultural change can therefore prove difficult, taking time, effort and perhaps sacrifice, but it can certainly be achieved.

All of these factors had to be taken into consideration when the culture of the Malays and other *bumiputeras* was changed so as to make it compatible with the requirements for economic success in the racially inequitable society found in Malaysia. Only specific, albeit important, aspects of their culture had to be changed, and to a large extent the process has been successfully carried out. But we are not yet out of the woods. More changes still need to be implemented or made truly effective.

By necessity, such changes must be deliberate and well thought out, as any correction in the prevailing culture can bring about serious and damaging side-effects. Thus a spiritually inclined society can become so materialistic and avaricious that its spiritual values are ignored or totally lost. Obviously, the need in Malaysia has been to retain the spiritual values, while balancing them with a reasonably materialistic creed. This is not easily done. Almost invariably, there will be a pendulum-like swing which may go too far in the other direction, with the total disappearance of any meaningful spiritual values. Therein lies the danger.

The change in values promoted to ensure the success of the NEP has to a large extent been effective. The culture of the peasant farmer, petty trader and hawker has largely been replaced by the more sophisticated culture of a commercial and industrial society. Change has proved to be possible. Admittedly, this has mostly taken place amongst the second generation of *bumiputeras*, a generation who are better educated and were never farmers, petty traders or hawkers. But the important factor is that the values which historically made up the *bumiputera* culture have been shown not to be inherent or permanent.

There are many lessons to be learned from the NEP. The methods used by the Malaysian Government to effect the metamorphosis of the *bumiputeras* from an agrarian and commercially unsophisticated people into a modern one, commercially oriented and capable of appreciating and applying science and technology, demonstrated that there is no inherent link between ethnicity or colour and material or spiritual achievements. If a determined attempt is made to change the culture to one suitable for the objective in mind, then, no matter how foreign or unusual the objective is, it can be achieved. The process is difficult and will take time, but some degree of success can be expected, even with the most backward people. It is not nature that stands in the way. What has happened is that, for some reason or other, a wrong turning was made during the development of the accepted culture. If there is a need to correct the direction, and that need is recognised, then the culture can be redirected and corrected.

The idea that skin colour determines the achievement or lack of achievement of a particular people is erroneous. There were perhaps more advanced black African civilisations before Christ than there were European ones. The Nubians and Ethiopians had already built up rich and extensive empires before the flowering of Egyptian civilisation. If the rest of black Africa remained primitive and backward, it was due to their cultures taking the wrong turning. Even then there is evidence of fairly sophisticated civilisations in many parts of black Africa.

In Europe the communists and socialists launched a new culture based on what they considered to be a better concept of justice for the human race. Their ideologues believed that, if the people were equally wealthy, human society would be perfect and just, and everyone would be contented. Communism was certainly not divinely inspired, finding its origins in what Marxists considered was pure rational thinking, a thinking devoid of any religion, or what Marx himself scathingly referred to as the 'opium of the masses'.

The benefit of hindsight has shown us that the new culture created by communists and socialists in Europe was a mistake, and certainly did not make people happier. The state replaced religion and other beliefs. The state cared for the people from birth, throughout life, and to death. Fear of death and the hereafter was regarded as mere superstition, which the scientific and logical mind must reject. The only entity to be feared was the state, even though the state was at the same time the provider of everything.

The culture of communism and socialism resulted in an empty civilisation. The initial joy at becoming equal with everyone else, if such an ideal was ever truly put into practice, soon wore off. Receiving the same wages, usually lower, for any kind or amount of work killed ambition and incentive. Diligence went unrewarded and the whole community became lazy. Productivity plummeted, in terms of both quantity and quality. The civilisation created by communist and socialist ethics and culture was not an improvement on earlier civilisations and cultures, whatever their shortcomings. It was a process of regression.

When a civilised society regresses, there must eventually be a move towards reform. A revolution against communism would probably have convulsed even the Soviet Union, if the communist leadership under Mikhail Gorbachev had not seen the danger signs and initiated reform. Gorbachev and the other reformers in eastern Europe obviously thought that by loosening the communist bondage, the people would be grateful and continue to accept their leadership. But they were wrong and the reformers went the same way as the hard-liners. They were rejected by the very people they had liberated.

Islam, on the other hand, represents an example of how a divinely inspired reform was able to transform a primitive people, given to tribalism and murderous feuding, into a highly cultured religious movement, which constructed a great civilisation and an empire stretching around the globe from Spain in the west to China in the east. The nomadic and quarrelsome Arab tribes of the Middle East united under Islam, after accepting the new ethics and values preached by the Prophet Muhammad, and began to imbibe and contribute towards the body of knowledge which has helped the development of human civilisation.

This transformation, which the primitive Arabs underwent once their value system had been changed, illustrates the influence of culture on the achievements of mankind. What is clear from this example alone is that even the most primitive of people can 'perform' if their values and ethics are right. Today, Muslim civilisation has regressed somewhat. Even the most casual observer cannot fail to relate this regression to the move away from the original values which Islam propagated. Where the Prophet preached unity and the brotherhood of the faithful, there is now total fragmentation, disunity and deep enmity within the Muslim *ummah*.

The NEP was a reaction to perceived injustice in Malaysian society. It was a relatively minor reform, not too radical or extreme, and, as we have seen, it succeeded. The reform succeeded because it could succeed. All mankind, irrespective of colour and creed, has the capacity and capability to succeed. What they need is direction, or redirection, a well-thought-out reformation of their culture, ethics and values, and eventually the further impetus of a rejuvenated civilisation.

Success will never be total. Even the changes and reforms divinely inspired were not completely successful. The good will always come together with the bad. But the idea that some people or race, due to their apparent backwardness and seemingly inferior culture, cannot change by assimilating a new set of values is clearly not valid. Everyone can change, by accepting and adopting new and correct values, and to some extent succeed. To make a success of the NEP, the culture, ethics and values of the Malays and the other *bumiputeras* had to be deliberately changed. They have remained recognisable as *bumiputeras*, but they have now become a new people, as capable as any other successful community in the world.

Cultural reformations involve whole human societies or nations. But what about individuals? Some individuals seem to be less well endowed than others. The fortunate few are extremely clever or very skilful, but others seem quite incapable of thinking logically, working out solutions to problems or learning something new. Is there any hope for them?

The answer is yes. Almost everyone has certain attributes and skills in which they can excel. The apparently less intelligent might shine in certain pursuits, where the so-called clever ones fail to do well or even acquire the basic skills. Thus an *orang asli* may not seem to possess great intellectual capacity, but, as was mentioned earlier, he can use his blowpipe to great effect, bringing down a monkey perched in a tree a hundred metres away. Einstein would probably have failed to hit anything at three metres!

Clearly, the *orang asli* have a special skill, apparently inherent, and developed to a very high degree. If another skill is introduced to the *orang asli*, and assiduously learned from an early age, there is no doubt that this new skill can be acquired. If the skill is acquired and practised as an integral part of their daily life, then in time, possibly over generations, the *orang asli* will develop the skill to a high degree, perhaps as high as their ability with the blowpipe. Eventually, the new skill will become a part of the common skills associated with the *orang asli*. If his values are correct, man will never cease striving, and will continue to develop his capabilities with every passing generation. The skills of our forefathers were inherited and improved upon by us, just as future generations will improve further what they inherit from us.

But what kind of skill is suitable for a man talented with a blowpipe? Handling survey instruments, measuring and, of course, shooting immediately spring to mind, and delicate work requiring a steady hand, such as in the assembly of electronic appliances. There are obviously many skills which an expert with the blowpipe can learn, provided he starts early enough in life and has a good teacher, and he and his people persist in learning, if necessary over a period of several generations.

The physical process has to be learned first and, over time, this becomes familiar. The objectives of doing the work will also be quickly assimilated. In time, the reasons and the rationale for acquiring the new skills will be understood. Finally, the complex scientific basis can be learned and mastered. This will all take time. Some individuals will acquire the new skills faster than others. But provided the discipline of learning is instilled, there really is nothing that cannot be learned by everyone, given sufficient time. The level of skill will, of course, differ between individuals, but this is perfectly natural.

The Malays and the other *bumiputeras* can acquire all the necessary skills and knowledge, given the will and the right impetus from their communities and the Government. There will be individuals who succeed all the way, and individuals who succeed part of the way. There will be some who seemingly fail, but they can be put to work learning other skills, more suited perhaps to their character and temperament. Certainly, their area of interest and outlook on life need no longer be confined to the old Malay world of the peasant farmer, petty trader and hawker. Provided nothing happens to change this course, future generations of *bumiputeras* can expect to become better and better in the areas of commerce and industry, and in other fields of knowledge. In short, the new culture that we are developing in Malaysia will be not only permanent, but enhanced with each passing generation.

The implementation of the NEP has undoubtedly changed the culture of the Malays and the other *bumiputeras*. They have acquired the culture of a modern commercial and industrial society. They remain *bumiputeras*, of course, but they are a new breed of people. As a result of this change, they have achieved economic success in commerce and industry, and have entered the mainstream of life in Malaysia. This has enabled the NEP largely to achieve its principal goals.